DISCOVER CREATION

DISCOVER CREATION

AN ILLUSTRATED ADVENTURE FOR KIDS

Tracy M. Sumner

BARBOUR **kidz**

A Division of Barbour Publishing

Previously published under the title *Kids' Guide to God's Creation*.

Print ISBN 978-1-64352-554-9

Published by Barbour Publishing, Inc., 1810 Barbour Drive, Uhrichsville, Ohio 44683, www.barbourbooks.com

Our mission is to inspire the world with the life-changing message of the Bible.

Printed in China.

001031 0222 HA

WHAT'S IN THIS BOOK

BEFORE YOU GET STARTED

Have you ever stopped to think about what the words "In the beginning God created" in Genesis 1:1 really mean? Just when was the beginning, and what did God create back then?

The simple but wonderful answer is that God created *everything*! And while only God knows exactly when the beginning took place, we can know without any doubt that He created a universe so big that people still don't know where it ends—or *if* it ends. He also created all the stars, including the one we call the sun. He created the planets that orbit the sun, including the planet we humans call home—Earth. And He created every living thing that lives here with us: every microbe, every plant, every fish, every bird, every mammal, every insect—the list goes on and on.

And, of course, He created us humans—the one thing He made in His own image and likeness—and designed us with the special ability to know and communicate with our Maker.

This book is about all the amazing things God created—starting with the heavens and the earth and ending with us humans. It's about the vastness of the universe God created, and it's about the amazing variety of things— things out there in outer space and things here on good old planet Earth— He made during those six days of work He spent creating everything you see. . .and some things you can't see.

Sometimes when we look at the wonder of God's creation, it's hard to fully comprehend that the God who lovingly and thoughtfully made everything—from the biggest galaxies, stars, and planets all the way down to the tiniest organisms (things you can't see with the naked eye) that live here on Earth—is the same God the Bible says loves each of us deeply and personally.

But the God who loves you is also the God who created everything around you. In fact, He created everything around you *for* you! It's true! Everything God made before He created us humans was with an eye toward preparing a place that would serve as a perfect home for each and every one of us. That's what the six days of creation were all about!

Some of God's creation is big and beautiful beyond description. Some of it is complicated and a little hard to understand. Some of it is funny to look at and think about. Some of it might even seem a little gross to you. But *all* of creation is amazing and wonderful—just like the God who used six days to accomplish all of it.

This book covers all six days of the creation story from the first chapter of Genesis. It gives you a fairly detailed day-by-day picture of what God made on each of those creation days. It covers the creation of the universe—or what some people call the *cosmos*—as well as the creation of the earth and everything that lives on it, including an incredible number of plants, animals, and other living things.

Each of the nine chapters in this book includes not only a good overview of the things God made on each creation day, but also some fun, interesting, and sometimes weird special features having to do with the chapter's main subject.

Here is a list of the features you'll enjoy in this book:

- **"That's Weird!"**: Really strange things within different parts of creation—like black holes in space, Venus flytraps (plants that eat meat), and the duck-billed platypus (quite possibly the world's weirdest mammal).

- **"Record Breaking"**: The biggest, the tallest, the farthest, and the most in all of creation!

- **"Exploring the. . ."**: Special experiments or studies you can do outside this book to learn more about the chapter's main topic.

- **"The Way It Used to Be"**: Really strange—and wrong—things people used to believe about different parts of God's creation.

- **"Did You Know. . . ?"**: Fun facts—some of them most people don't know—about the natural world God created.

- **"That's Amazing!"**: Some really astounding tidbits about the universe, the earth, and the natural world that makes its home on our planet.

This book won't teach you everything there is to know about the universe and the world God created for you to live on—or about the living things we share our planet with. For you to learn about every single thing God created, you would need a book many times longer than the one you're holding in your hands right now.

But by the time you're finished reading this book, you will have a pretty good idea of how big and wonderful creation really is—and how big and wonderful the God who made it all is too. You also might find yourself wanting to read and study to learn more! When you do that, you'll learn not only about the wonder of God's creation, but you'll also learn a thing or two about God Himself that you might not have known before.

GENESIS 1: THE CREATION STORY

¹ In the beginning God created the heavens and the earth. ² The earth was formless and empty, and darkness covered the deep waters. And the Spirit of God was hovering over the surface of the waters.

³ Then God said, "Let there be light," and there was light. ⁴ And God saw that the light was good. Then he separated the light from the darkness. ⁵ God called the light "day" and the darkness "night."

And evening passed and morning came, marking the first day.

⁶ Then God said, "Let there be a space between the waters, to separate the waters of the heavens from the waters of the earth." ⁷ And that is what happened. God made this space to separate the waters of the earth from the waters of the heavens. ⁸ God called the space "sky."

And evening passed and morning came, marking the second day.

⁹ Then God said, "Let the waters beneath the sky flow together into one place, so dry ground may appear." And that is what happened. ¹⁰ God called the dry ground "land" and the waters "seas." And God saw that it was good. ¹¹ Then God said, "Let the land sprout with vegetation—every sort of seed-bearing plant, and trees that grow seed-bearing fruit. These seeds will then produce the kinds of plants and trees from which they came." And that is what happened. ¹² The land produced vegetation—all sorts of seed-bearing plants, and trees with seed-bearing fruit. Their seeds produced plants and trees of the same kind. And God saw that it was good.

¹³ And evening passed and morning came, marking the third day.

¹⁴ Then God said, "Let lights appear in the sky to separate the day from the night. Let them be signs to mark the seasons, days, and years. ¹⁵ Let these lights in the sky shine down on the earth." And that is what happened. ¹⁶ God made two great lights—the larger one to govern the day, and the smaller one to govern the night. He also made the stars. ¹⁷ God set these lights in the sky to light the earth, ¹⁸ to govern the day and night, and to separate the light from the darkness. And God saw that it was good.

¹⁹ And evening passed and morning came, marking the fourth day.

²⁰ Then God said, "Let the waters swarm with fish and other life. Let the skies be filled with birds of every kind." ²¹ So God created great sea creatures and every living thing that scurries and swarms in the water, and every sort of bird—each producing offspring of the same kind. And God saw that it was good. ²² Then God blessed them, saying, "Be fruitful and multiply. Let the fish fill the seas, and let the birds multiply on the earth."

²³ And evening passed and morning came, marking the fifth day.

²⁴ Then God said, "Let the earth produce every sort of animal, each producing offspring of the same kind—livestock, small animals that scurry along the ground, and wild animals." And that is what happened. ²⁵ God made all sorts of wild animals, livestock, and small animals, each able to produce offspring of the same kind. And God saw that it was good.

²⁶ Then God said, "Let us make human beings in our image, to be like us. They will reign over the fish in the sea, the birds in the sky, the livestock, all the wild animals on the earth, and the small animals that scurry along the ground."

²⁷ So God created human beings in his own image. In the image of God he created them; male and female he created them.

²⁸ Then God blessed them and said, "Be fruitful and multiply. Fill the earth and govern it. Reign over the fish in the sea, the birds in the sky, and all the animals that scurry along the ground."

²⁹ Then God said, "Look! I have given you every seed-bearing plant throughout the earth and all the fruit trees for your food. ³⁰ And I have given every green plant as food for all the wild animals, the birds in the sky, and the small animals that scurry along the ground—everything that has life." And that is what happened.

³¹ Then God looked over all he had made, and he saw that it was very good!

And evening passed and morning came, marking the sixth day.

CHAPTER 1

DAY 1, PART I
HOW IT ALL STARTED— HEAVENS, EARTH, AND WATER

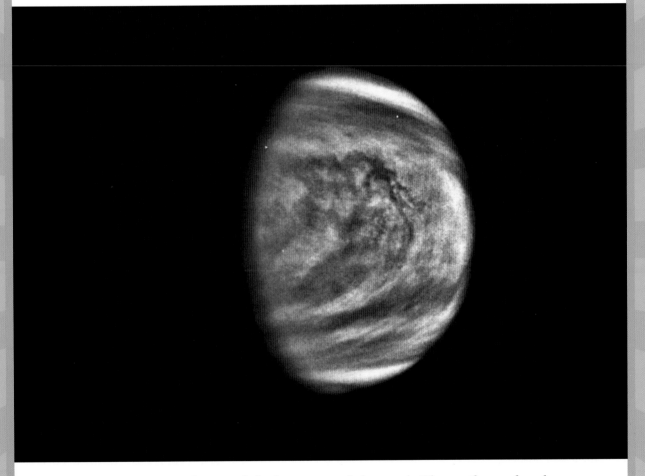

In the beginning God created the heavens and the earth. The earth was formless and empty, and darkness covered the deep waters. And the Spirit of God was hovering over the surface of the waters.

GENESIS 1:1–2

Have you ever really thought about the word *nothing*? When you look around you and see all the really cool things God created, it's hard to imagine that there was a time when there was literally nothing around—no Earth, no moon, no stars, no people, no animals, and no plants. There wasn't even a place for God to put all these things! What's more, there wasn't even any light!

The Bible tells us that God's work of creation began in the same place everything else begins: in the *beginning*! Before that day, the only thing that existed was God Himself. And on that first day of creation, He began laying the foundation for everything you see around you—and for a lot of things you can't see.

The Bible tells us, "In the beginning God created the heavens and the earth" (Genesis 1:1). That certainly seems like a good place to start, doesn't it? But the earth God started creating on the first day of creation wasn't at all like the earth you see around you now—at least not at first. The Bible tells us that at the beginning of creation, "the earth was formless and empty" (Genesis 1:2).

What does the phrase "formless and empty" sound like to you? It certainly doesn't sound like the earth would have been a very pleasant place to live back then, does it? In fact, it sounds like the earth was nothing but a huge ball of gases and solid materials that no human, animal, or plant could possibly live on. It sounds like it was more or less a big unformed blob of what God later molded and formed into the amazing planet Earth you live on now. Some people believe that on the first day of creation, God made what scientists call *matter*. Matter is basically all the materials God would later need to get the work of creation going.

One of the basic laws of science is that you can't make something out of nothing. But God can! And that's exactly what He did! On that first day of creation, God began an amazing process of putting together everything we see around us—starting with what the Bible calls "the heavens and the earth" (Genesis 1:1).

The Heavens—a Huge Area We Call Space

What the Bible calls "the heavens" in Genesis 1, we now call *space* or the *universe* or the *cosmos*. This is a huge area God created on that first day, then later filled with planets, stars, and other amazing things you'll read about later on in chapter 5.

But just how big is the universe? About 500 years ago, people believed the entire universe was only a little bigger than Earth. And it wasn't all that long ago when schoolchildren were taught that the universe is maybe only about 5,000 light-years across—much smaller than scientists have since discovered it really is. Today, when modern technology allows us to see deeper into the universe, we have learned that space is much bigger than anyone in the past could have possibly imagined.

It's hard for most of us to imagine just how big the universe really is. In fact, even the smartest scientists in the world today really don't know the exact size of outer space. Over the past few decades, scientists have come to believe the universe actually had a beginning (just like the Bible says it does) and that it is still growing and expanding. That means we may never know just how big it is—simply because the universe God created is still getting bigger all the time.

For now, scientists know that outer space extends away from Earth by at least 13 billion light-years. A *light-year* is how far light—which travels at about 186,000 miles per second—moves in one year. So you know that the distance between Earth and the farthest objects humans have seen out in space is probably far too huge for you to figure out with a pencil and paper—even if you're really good at arithmetic!

The visible universe covers an area that is about 28 billion light-years across. Scientists know that they are limited in what they can see in space, but they believe it's possible that what they have seen so far could actually make up a small fraction of the whole universe.

Even though the universe is bigger than most people can even imagine, you can know one thing about it for sure: Every inch of it was created by the same God who so carefully and thoughtfully created you and every other person who lives here on Earth, or who has ever lived here on Earth. And He's the same God who made sure during the process of creation that you would have everything you need to live your life here on Earth.

Most everyone has seen a magician make a rabbit appear from an empty hat. But you know it's just a trick. Only God can make something from nothing!

The Hubble Space Telescope floats more than 350 miles above the earth. From that far up, beyond Earth's atmosphere, the Hubble can take clear pictures of deep space objects.

What It's Really Like in Space

What do you think it's like in outer space—thousands or millions of miles away from Earth? Is it really cold out there, or is it really hot? What does outer space sound like? What could you see if you suddenly found yourself floating around in outer space?

When you think of outer space, you probably imagine a huge area filled with stars, planets, asteroids, comets, and other objects zipping around one another at light speed—and making lots of noise as they do it. But even though countless numbers of objects like these are out there, outer space isn't really all that crowded. Most of the objects we can see in space are many, many light-years apart, and even those objects that are relatively close to one another very seldom come all that close to one another.

And outer space is anything but noisy. In fact, it's the quietest place in all creation.

Have you ever seen one of those old science-fiction movies where a spaceship explodes and

As of now, the farthest we've seen into space is more than 13 billion light-years away. That tells us that the heavens God created are bigger than most of us can imagine! But as huge as outer space is, the farthest any human being has traveled in space is to our

moon, which is about 250,000 miles from Earth. On July 20, 1969, the spacecraft *Apollo 11*, which was commanded by Neil Armstrong, achieved the first manned landing on the moon's surface. Armstrong was the first to set foot on the moon, followed by Buzz Aldrin. After that mission, the United States' National Aeronautics and Space Administration (NASA) carried out five more manned moon landings, the last of which was in 1972.

One of the twelve humans to walk on the moon explores a deep hole called the Plum Crater. Notice the electric-powered "moon buggy" in the background. Look like fun?

gives off a loud *bang*? Outer-space explosions in movies can look and sound pretty cool. But did you know that if a blast like that happened in outer space, it wouldn't give off any sound at all?

In order for sound to travel, it has to have something to travel through. Sound travels by causing tiny particles of air—called *molecules*—to vibrate. Of course, sound can also travel through other kinds of molecules, like water, and even some solid objects like wood or metal. On Earth, where there is air, sound travels to your ears through vibrating air. But since there is no air or atmosphere of any kind in space, sound waves can't travel there.

Light, on the other hand, *can* travel through space. If you want quick proof, all you have to do is look up in the sky at night and see the stars. The light from those stars traveled many millions of miles before it reached Earth. Light can travel through space because it doesn't have to travel through anything like air or other matter. So if you were in outer space and a spaceship exploded, you could see the flash but you wouldn't hear the sound of the explosion.

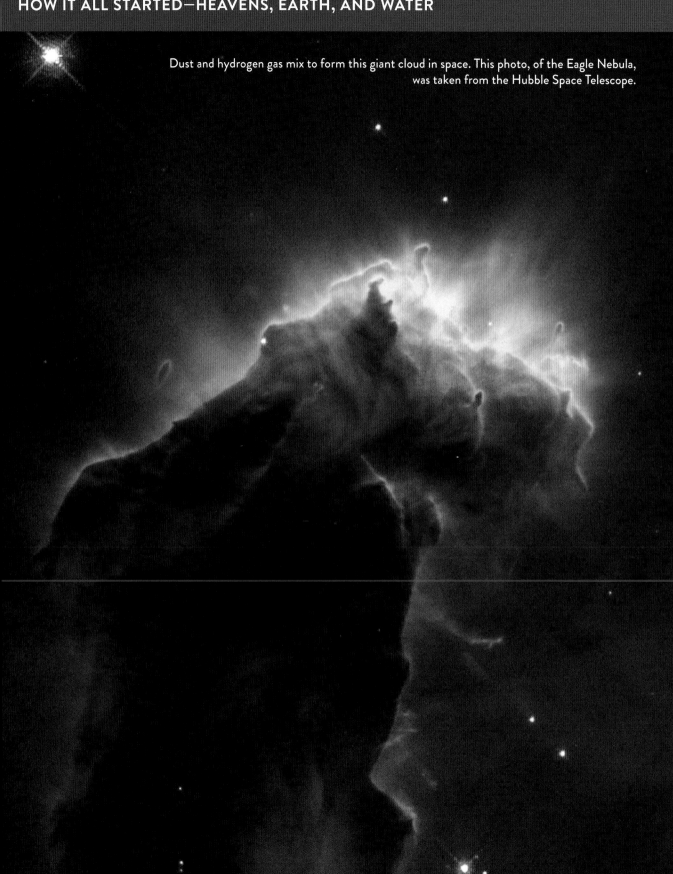

Dust and hydrogen gas mix to form this giant cloud in space. This photo, of the Eagle Nebula, was taken from the Hubble Space Telescope.

Even though outer space isn't crowded with big objects bumping into one another, it is not really empty, either. Some of the huge gaps between planets and stars and other bodies in space are filled with huge amounts of gas and dust. A lot of that gas and dust is spread very thin in space. Some of it appears only as atoms or molecules. There are also many kinds of radiation in space. The sun gives off many kinds of radiation that make their way through space and arrive here on Earth. Some of the radiation in space is necessary for life on Earth.

The Size and Shape of Planet Earth

The planet you live on might seem pretty big to you, but compared with the rest of the universe God created, Earth is like a tiny speck of sand on a huge, sand dune–covered beach. The universe is that big!

But just how big is the earth? Actually, that depends on how you measure it. The earth's *diameter* (how wide it is) is about 7,900 miles, and its *circumference* (how big around it is) is about 24,900 miles. The earth's *radius* (the distance between the surface of the earth all the way down to its center) is about 4,000 miles. The earth's total surface area—including both land and water—is almost 197 million square miles.

Earth is huge to us but just a tiny part of the whole universe.

THAT'S AMAZING!

Eratosthenes of Cyrene

It might amaze you to know this, but people who lived before the time of Jesus had a pretty good idea of the earth's actual size. In about 200 BC, a Greek mathematician named Eratosthenes of Cyrene used the altitude of the sun in the sky on the first day of summer (the *summer solstice*) in a city called Syene (now Aswan, Egypt) and in Alexandria, Egypt, which was about 490 miles north of Syene, to calculate that the earth's circumference was about 25,000 miles. He was off by less than 100 miles!

While you probably didn't know how big around or how wide the earth is, you probably know that the earth is round. Or is it?

Actually, the earth isn't perfectly round, even though the globe in your school classroom—or maybe the one you have in your own bedroom—makes it look that way. Scientists call our planet an *oblate spheroid* because it bulges a little bit at the equator, which is the line that circles the earth and separates the Northern Hemisphere from the Southern Hemisphere. The earth is about 42 miles bigger around at the equator than it is when measured around from north to south.

That means that the earth isn't shaped like a fully inflated basketball but more like that same basketball if you let some of the air out of it, put it on the floor, and then lightly pressed down on it from the top.

THE WAY IT USED TO BE

One of the first things you probably learned in school about the earth is that it is round. But people didn't always believe that. Thousands of years ago, almost everyone believed that the earth was flat like a piece of paper and not round like a basketball. That began to change in the fourth century BC, when Greek scientists and philosophers—including Aristotle, one of the first to provide real evidence that the earth was not flat—began to teach that the earth was a sphere (like a basketball), or at least round in shape.

The Layers of the Earth

If you were to look at a cross-section of the earth—in other words, split it in half so you could see what is inside—you'd see that the earth is made of four different layers, sort of like the layers of an onion. The outermost layer of the earth is called the *crust.*

The earth's crust is about 25 miles thick underneath land but only about 6.5 miles thick underneath the oceans. The earth's crust is made up of relatively light and brittle materials that can crack during earthquakes. There are about 90 known elements in the earth's crust, and they combine in several natural ways to create materials known as *minerals.* There are about 3,700 known minerals in the earth's crust.

Underneath the earth's crust is what is called the *mantle.* The earth's mantle is the thickest layer of the four. It extends from the

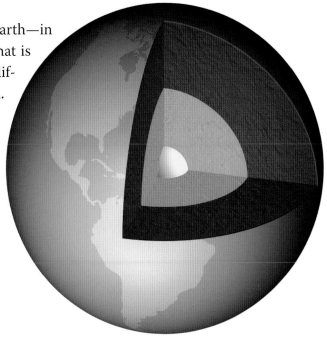

Earth's four layers are seen in this cross-section diagram— the crust, or thin outer layer; the mantle, in brown; the outer core, in orange; and the inner core, in yellow.

bottom of the crust all the way down into the earth about 1,800 miles. The mantle is made up of thick, solid, rocky materials that make up about 85 percent of the earth's weight and mass. Scientists believe the first 50 miles or so of the mantle are made up of very hard rock. The 150 miles after that are made up of very hot (an estimated 4,000 to 6,700 degrees Fahrenheit) rock. The rest of the mantle is made up of very solid, strong rocky materials.

The next layer of the earth after the mantle is the *outer core.* The outer core is about 3,000 miles beneath the surface. Scientists believe the outer core is made up of very hot (about 6,700 degrees Fahrenheit) liquid metals—mostly iron and nickel. The earth's *inner core* is also very hot (around 6,700 to 8,500 degrees Fahrenheit) and is also made mostly of iron and nickel, but it is under such pressure that it is completely solid.

DID YOU KNOW. . . ?

The earth itself—not counting its atmosphere—is made up of several elements. *Elements* are substances that cannot be broken down by any natural chemical means. They are the basic building blocks of everything around us. The earth is made up of about 34.6 percent iron (most of which is in the inner layers of the earth), 29.5 percent oxygen, 15.2 percent silicon, 12.7 percent magnesium, 2.4 percent nickel, 1.9 percent sulfur, and .05 percent titanium.

The Earth's Surface—a Huge Jigsaw Puzzle

When you look at a map of the earth, you might get the idea that its surface is one solid shell that covers the entire planet. But the earth's crust is not one big solid outer layer. It is actually broken up into several huge, thick plates that sit on top of the earth's mantle. These plates are made of rock, and they are about 50 to 250 miles thick.

The seven largest of these plates are the African plate, the Eurasian plate (under Europe and Asia), the North American plate, the South American plate, the Australian plate, the Antarctic plate, and the Pacific plate. There are also several other smaller plates on the earth's surface, including the Arabian, Nazca, and Philippine plates. The places where the plates meet one another are called *plate boundaries.*

These plates don't just sit in one place. They move both sideways in different directions and up and down. The plates move very slowly—from under an inch to a few inches every year, depending on which plate it is. Sometimes the plates move away from each other, but sometimes they crash together or brush one another as they move. Most of the earth's volcanoes and earthquakes (what scientists call *seismic activity*) happen when the earth's plates move away from, toward, or into one another.

Earthquakes can be so small that hardly anyone feels them—or so strong that they cause buildings to collapse.

The Gift of Water

Earth is a one-of-a-kind creation because it is the only planet in our solar system—which includes our sun and the other planets that orbit it—known to have liquid water, which is absolutely necessary for the survival of all known life-forms.

About 71 percent (almost three-quarters) of our earth's surface is covered with saltwater oceans. Continents and islands—as well as the freshwater rivers, lakes, and streams found on them—make up the rest of the earth's surface.

Scientists estimate that there are more than 326 million *trillion* gallons of water on our planet. That's an awful lot of water! But where do you think all that water is at any given time? If you guessed that most of it is in the oceans, you'd be right! Around 97 percent of the earth's water at any given time is in the oceans, seas, and bays. Less than 3 percent of the earth's water is fresh water, and most of that water is found in ice caps, glaciers, and other frozen forms.

Though you can see the evidence of water in our atmosphere in the form of clouds, the amount of water in the atmosphere (.001 percent) is a very small part of the total water on Earth. It might surprise you to know that the world's freshwater lakes and rivers also account for a very small amount of the total water on Earth.

A scuba diver skims through the clear blue water of the Caribbean Sea.

Even though there is an amazing amount of water on the earth's surface, a small percentage of it is drinkable. Most of the earth's water is found in seas and oceans—about 97 percent—and is too salty to drink. Another 2 percent is frozen in ice caps and glaciers. That leaves less than 1 percent of all the water on Earth that is fresh and clean enough for humans and animals to drink.

What's So Important about Water?

When God created the earth, He made sure that the people, animals, and plants He created it for would have everything they needed to live, grow, and reproduce. That included the most common—and most important—substance in the world: water!

Without water, life as we know it on Earth simply can't exist. Many kinds of plants and animals live in the water, but they aren't the only ones who need water to live. People, as well as all land animals, plants, and other living things, must have water to survive. In fact, we humans can live for weeks without eating food, but we would survive less than seven days without water.

Water is important to all living things because it has the ability to dissolve other substances. That helps water to carry needed nutrients to cells and to carry waste away from them. The bodies of almost all living things are more than half water. Some organisms' bodies are up to 95 percent water. Water makes up about 60 to 70 percent of the weight of your body and about 83 percent of your blood is water. Even your bones are 25 percent water! The human brain weighs about 3 pounds, but if you squeezed all the water out of your brain, it would weigh only 10 ounces.

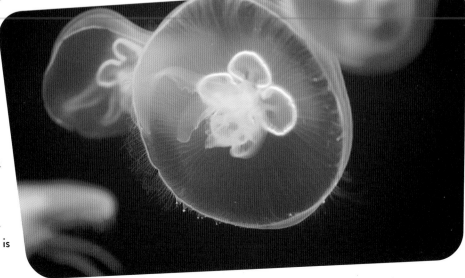

Jellyfish are approximately 95 percent water. This one is called a *moon jellyfish*.

The Wonder of Water

You've probably heard water called H_2O. Have you ever wondered what that means? When you look at a glass of water, what you're seeing is millions of tiny particles of water called *water molecules.* Each water molecule is made up of two atoms of hydrogen (the H_2 part) and one atom of oxygen (the O part).

You'd need a very good microscope to see what this model imitates—two hydrogen atoms attached to an oxygen atom, making up a molecule of water.

When these three atoms come together to form a water molecule, the bond is very hard to break. That is partly why nearly all the water on Earth now has been here since the beginning of creation. That means that the water we are using today is the same water that people all through history used and the same water the animals God first created used. Just think! Someone famous in history may have bathed in the very same water that you brushed your teeth with this morning! (Don't worry. . .all the *impurities*—the gross stuff you wouldn't want to put in your mouth—are long gone, so when you use water from your tap to brush your teeth, you're using just the water.)

Today we find water on Earth in three forms. Water appears as a *liquid* (just plain water), as a *solid* (ice), and as a *gas* (steam or water vapor). The fact that water can take on these three forms helps the earth to distribute its water through ocean currents, through the movement of ice, and through precipitation (rain and snow).

Water appears in its three forms—liquid, solid, and gas—off Greenland.

In its natural form, water freezes and takes on solid form at 32 degrees Fahrenheit. Water boils and begins to turn to gas at 212 degrees Fahrenheit. But water doesn't have to reach 212 degrees Fahrenheit to be turned to gas or vapor. Water also turns to vapor in the form of clouds and fog when water from the ocean evaporates and forms tiny water droplets. The tiny droplets of water are invisible until they condense enough in the atmosphere to form clouds and fog.

THAT'S WEIRD!

Water really is an amazing substance. You may have learned in school that water is the only material on Earth that exists as a solid, liquid, and a gas in natural conditions on our planet. But in the right conditions, water can actually take on other forms. When water is cooled down very quickly to colder than around negative 184 degrees Fahrenheit, a weird thing happens: The water turns to the thickness of molasses. At negative 211, the water turns solid but has no crystal structure, like normal ice has. Scientists call this phenomenon *glassy water*—because the frozen water is completely clear, just like glass.

CHAPTER 2

DAY 1, PART II
LET THERE BE LIGHT!

Then God said, "Let there be light," and there was light. And God saw that the light was good. Then he separated the light from the darkness. God called the light "day" and the darkness "night." And evening passed and morning came, marking the first day.

GENESIS 1:3–5

Can you imagine being in a place where there is absolutely no light? We're not talking about the kind of darkness you can experience on a really dark night away from the city lights when the moon isn't shining overhead. That's dark, but it's not *absolute* darkness because there is always some light. (If you're ever out on a night like that, you'll find that your eyes will adjust and you will be able to see at least a little bit.) We're talking about absolute blackness—the kind where you literally can't see your hand in front of your face.

The Bible says that in the beginning, "darkness covered the deep waters" (Genesis 1:2). This was before God created light of any kind, so it's easy to imagine that creation up to that point was covered in absolute darkness. Not only wasn't there much to be seen (remember, the earth was just a formless mass at that time), there wasn't even any light to see it!

It wasn't long before God put a stop to that incredible darkness by simply speaking the words "Let there be light." In an instant, God had taken that first step in preparing the earth as a suitable place for people, plants, and animals to live on. Not only would the light God created allow us humans and the animals to see, but it would also be the basis for all life on planet Earth.

The sun helps plants to grow. . .and the plants help you to grow!

Why Light Is Important

How would you answer if someone were to ask you why light is important? Probably the first thing that would come to your mind is that you need light to see! But let's imagine for a moment that every living thing on Earth—including us humans—had every sense we have now. . . except sight. Would light still be important to us? If so, *how* would it be important?

Light, which comes from the sun to the earth, is an absolute necessity for everything that lives here. Without light, nothing could live on Earth. That includes the plants and animals that live above ground, as well as the ones that live underground. And it includes people!

One reason light is important is because plants need it to grow and produce energy—or food. This happens during a process called *photosynthesis*, which you'll read more about in chapter 4. Plants are the foundation of all food here on Earth. All animals on Earth eat either plants or other animals that eat plants. Without light, plants would stop growing and die, and if that happened, all other life here on Earth, including humans, would soon die of starvation.

Light from the sun is also important because it heats the earth. Without the sun's light, there wouldn't be enough energy on Earth to keep us warm enough to live here. God placed our planet just the right distance from the sun to allow its light to heat our atmosphere to just the right temperature.

When God created light, He created the foundation for all the life He would later carefully design to live here on Earth. God thought far enough ahead in His plan of creation to know that before any living things could be placed here on Earth, there had to be light to support them and feed them.

THAT'S WEIRD!

As crazy as it may sound, scientists have proved that light itself can be bent or moved by intense gravity from objects such as stars. Gravity can also change the energy of light. The astrophysicist Sir Arthur Eddington proved the effect of gravity on light during a solar eclipse in 1919. With the sun completely blocked and the sky dark enough to see stars, Eddington photographed the stars that appeared close to the sun in the sky and observed that their light had actually been bent as it passed by the sun.

In a total solar eclipse, the moon almost exactly blocks the sun, leaving only the sun's "crown" (or corona) in view.

What Is Light Really?

Maybe all you really understand about light is that you need it in order not to trip over things when you walk into a room. When you walk into your bedroom at night, the first thing you probably do is reach for a light switch so you can see where you're going.

But there's a lot more to light than just how it allows us to see things. Light is a fascinating creation of God that has some amazing scientific properties—some of which you probably never even thought of before.

Light is sometimes called *radiant energy* or *electromagnetic energy* because it is both electric and magnetic. There are many kinds of light. There is the light you can see, and there is light you can't see—like gamma rays, X-rays, ultraviolet light, and radio waves. While you may not have thought of some of these things as light, by all scientific definitions, they really are forms of light.

Sir Isaac Newton (1642–1727)

For centuries, people argued over whether light travels as a *wave* (like waves in water, only without what scientists call a *medium*) or as *particles* (like tiny pellets from a shotgun blast). In the seventeenth century (about 400 years ago), the great English scientist Sir Isaac Newton studied light and came to the conclusion that it was more or less a stream of particles (he called them *corpuscles*). Around that same time, another great scientist named Christiaan Huygens, who lived and worked in Holland, taught that light traveled in waves.

As it turns out, they were both right!

During the twentieth century, scientists started to believe and teach that light travels as both particles and waves. This idea is called *wave-particle duality*. Scientists began believing this because light behaves like a wave in some ways and like a particle in others. They call the particles of light *quanta*—which is plural for *quantum*—or *photons*.

Christiaan Huygens (1629–1695)

How Light Travels. . .and What It Does When It Gets Here

When you're outside on a sunny day, you probably don't think much about how the sunlight you're enjoying made it through space to Earth. But sunlight doesn't just leave the sun and arrive here on Earth in an instant. In fact, the light and warmth you feel from the sun actually left the sun's surface about 8 minutes, 18 seconds before it reached you.

Light travels through space at about 186,000 miles per second. When light leaves the sun, it travels in a straight line—in all directions. But when it hits something either here on Earth or somewhere else—even air—it starts to act very differently. And you can be thankful that it does!

When it comes to your ability to see things, the most important thing light does when it runs into things is reflect. If it weren't for reflection, you couldn't see anything around you. That's because when light hits something here on Earth—a person, a car, a tree. . .anything you can imagine—it bounces, or reflects, off that object and into your eyes, allowing you to see it. If light were somehow stopped from reflecting off things, they would still be there, but you wouldn't be able to see them.

The speed and direction of light also changes when it runs into materials like water, glass, or plastic. When light waves hit these materials, they slow down and bend. This is called *refraction*. You can see the effects of refraction when you look at someone standing waist-deep in the water in a swimming pool. From where you stand, it looks like the water has changed the angle of the person's legs. But the water hasn't done anything at all to that person; it's just that light bends and changes direction when it hits water, and that makes it look like the person's legs have been bent at the wrong angle.

Humans have made great use of the refraction of light. For example, the lenses of eyeglasses, which are usually made of glass or plastic, are curved enough to refract (or bend) the light that enters a person's eyes and allow him or her to see things more clearly than he or she could without glasses. Refraction is also used in cameras, binoculars, camcorders, and other things designed with lenses.

Light refraction can "enlarge" what you're looking at—which is why Sherlock Holmes used a magnifying glass to look for clues.

Why Is There Color? Because of Light!

One of the coolest things about light is that it allows us to see different colors. But did you know that light itself is actually a big collection of colors? It's true! If there were no colors in light, especially sunlight, you wouldn't be able to see any colors at all.

Here's a quick explanation of how color comes from light.

Light waves come in many different frequencies. The *frequency of light* is the number of light waves that pass through a certain point during a certain time period—usually one second.

Imagine that light waves are like waves in the ocean. Waves in water have a *crest* (a high point) and a *trough* (a low point). Depending on how the wave started, these crests and troughs can be of different sizes and can be farther apart or closer together. The same thing is true of light. In light, the distance between the crests and troughs is called the *amplitude,* and it determines the light's brightness. The distance between the crests of each wave is called the *wavelength,* and it determines the light's color.

If you could see the actual waves of light, you would see that *low frequency* light waves are a lot like slow, rolling waves in water—with more distance between each wave's peaks. *High frequency* light waves are like higher waves in water with less distance between them.

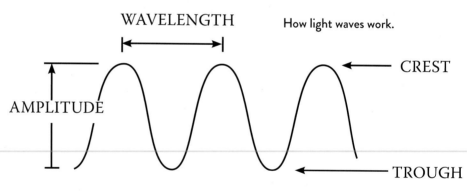

WAVELENGTH

How light waves work.

AMPLITUDE

CREST

TROUGH

Low frequency light has lower energy, and high frequency light has higher energy. The light with the highest frequency are *gamma rays,* and the light with the lowest frequency are *radio waves*—both of which are invisible to the human eye. The visible light with the highest frequency is *violet light,* and the visible light with the lowest frequency is *red light.*

Your eyes can only see light that is more or less in the middle of the frequency spectrum. This range is called the *visible spectrum* or *visible light.* You can't see infrared light because it is just below the frequency of the visible spectrum, and you can't see ultraviolet light because it is just above the visible spectrum.

Your eye can tell apart around 10,000 different colors or shades of visible light. For example, you can see many different shades of each color. Most of the time, though, the visible spectrum of light is made up of a list of the seven major colors you can see in a rainbow. In order from the longest wavelength to the shortest, these colors are red, orange, yellow, green, blue, indigo, and violet. This list is often referred to as ROY G. BIV (go back and write down the first letter in each color of the rainbow in order, and you'll see why).

THAT'S WEIRD!

All electromagnetic radiation is considered light, but we humans can only see the light that is within a certain frequency or wavelength. But that doesn't mean that light we humans can't see is invisible to every living thing on planet Earth. Scientists have somehow figured out that certain kinds of reptiles can see infrared light and that many fish, reptiles, birds, and insects can see ultraviolet light. Both of these frequencies of light come from the sun, and both are completely invisible to us humans.

Antiterrorist police are shown through a night-vision device. It uses nonvisible light to help people see in the darkness.

God created the rainbow as a promise never again to flood the entire earth. See the whole story in Genesis 9:12–15.

How We See Colors

When you see sunlight on your hand or on some other object, it looks like it's pretty much one color—kind of yellowish white. That is why sunlight is sometimes called *white light.* But in reality, sunlight is made up of all the different colors all mixed together. When you look at a rainbow, what you're seeing is droplets of water splitting sunlight into its different colors by bending (or refracting) different colors of light.

So how do we see different colors here on Earth? Why is an apple red? Why are the leaves on plants green? It has a lot to do with how different things react to sunlight, and it also has to do with how our eyes receive light and color.

When sunlight hits a red apple, the red part of the sunlight is reflected off the apple's peel, while other colors are absorbed into the apple's skin so that you can't see them. On the other hand, if you were to look at the same red apple with sunlight shining on it that had been filtered through a piece of green plastic, the apple wouldn't appear red but would look black or gray. That's because the apple absorbed the green light instead of reflecting it back to you.

Everything on Earth is designed in such a way that it absorbs certain colors of light but reflects others. That's as true of your skin and hair and eyes as it is of green plants, red apples, and anything else on Earth that we see as having a particular color.

THAT'S AMAZING!

The first person to prove that sunlight is a mixture of all colors was Sir Isaac Newton, the great seventeenth-century English scientist. Newton passed sunlight through a glass prism to separate the colors into a rainbow spectrum. He then took a second prism and a lens and combined the two rainbows. You might think that the result was one big rainbow of colors, but you'd be wrong. What Newton produced when he combined the two spectrums was white light. This proved that white light isn't just white but is a mixture of light of many different colors or frequencies.

The First Day and the First Night

When God created light on that first day of creation, He also separated the times when it was dark outside and when it was light. Another way to say that is to say that God created night and day. Even though God wouldn't make the sun until the fourth day of creation, He started things out on the first day by designing the earth and light so that there would be night and day once about every twenty-four hours.

People use the terms *sunrise* and *sunset* to describe the daily appearance and disappearance of the sun. But in reality, the sun doesn't rise or set at all. The sun mostly stays in the same place—at least in relation to the earth—all the time. So when you see the sun appear in the east every morning and disappear in the west every evening, it's because the earth is spinning on an axis as it orbits (or circles) the sun. In other words, it's the earth that is moving in relation to the sun, not the other way around.

When it's dark outside where you live, it's because the sun is shining on the other side of the earth. That means that it's always daylight somewhere on Earth and that while you are sleeping, people on the other side of the world are busy doing some of the same kinds of things you do when it's daytime where you live.

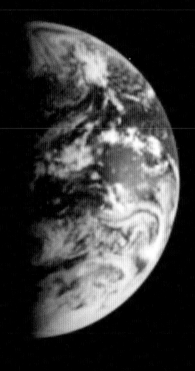

The *Galileo* spacecraft took this picture of earth—half bathed in the light of the sun—from almost four million miles away!

One tradition says that in leap years, a woman can propose marriage to a man. This postcard, from more than 100 years ago, has some fun with that idea.

If someone were to ask you how long it takes the earth to *rotate* (make one complete spin) on its axis (in other words, how long a day on Earth lasts), you'd probably answer, "Everyone knows it's 24 hours!" But the earth doesn't rotate quite that long. It actually takes the earth only 23 hours, 56 minutes to completely rotate in relation to the sun. But here's another interesting fact: The time it takes the earth to *orbit* (or circle) the sun is actually a little more than a 365-day calendar year. The earth actually orbits the sun once every 365 days plus one-quarter of a day. That's why we have a February 29 once every four years in what is called a *leap year*.

When God Created Time

Even though all Christians agree that God created the earth and everything in and around it, some of them disagree over how long it took God to do it. Some believe the earth is very young—between 6,000 and 10,000 years old—while others believe the earth is very old. . .maybe billions of years old.

People will probably never completely agree on the answer to the question of how old the earth really is—at least not in this lifetime. But one thing we can probably all agree on is that God actually created time as we know it on the first day of creation when He separated day from night.

Has anyone ever asked you to define the word *time*? It's probably not as easy as you think! People mostly think of time in terms of seconds, minutes, hours, days, and years. But those are just *measurements* of time. It's hard to define time, so we'll just say that *time* is the means people use to measure the periods between certain events.

Probably the most basic measurement of time is the day. Since each day has a certain amount of daytime and a certain amount of nighttime, people use 24-hour days to measure time. But time is also measured by years. On Earth a year is measured by the time it takes for the earth to completely orbit the sun. But even that measurement of time isn't perfect. You see, a year on Earth doesn't last exactly 365 days but about 365 days and 6 hours.

We humans are limited by time. We all begin our time on Earth when we are born, and one day our time on Earth will end. Not so with the God who began the process of making everything around us on that first day of creation. God exists outside the bounds of time. God is eternal. That means that He has always existed and will always exist. And when He created time on the first day, it was just the beginning of the process of showing His own greatness and love through making everything you see around you.

CHAPTER 3

DAY 2
OUR EARTH'S ATMOSPHERE

Then God said, "Let there be a space between the waters, to separate the waters of the heavens from the waters of the earth." And that is what happened. God made this space to separate the waters of the earth from the waters of the heavens. God called the space "sky." And evening passed and morning came, marking the second day.

GENESIS 1:6–8

You probably don't give a lot of thought to air when you take a deep breath, but the air you breathe is part of what makes it possible for you—and every other person and every other living thing—to live here on Earth.

Another word for the air you breathe is *atmosphere.* Earth's atmosphere is made up of three main gases: *nitrogen, oxygen,* and *argon.* About 78 percent (more than three-quarters) of our atmosphere is made up of nitrogen, with oxygen accounting for about 21 percent. Argon accounts for a little less than 1 percent of our planet's atmosphere, with the remainder made up of carbon dioxide and small traces of other gases. In addition to the gases in our atmosphere, there are also small particles of dust, water, and pollen floating around.

When you breathe in air, you breathe in everything that's in it. Nitrogen and argon are what are called *inert gases*, which means they don't react chemically with other substances. So when the nitrogen and argon enter your lungs when you inhale, they do an about-face and leave your lungs when you exhale. . .without affecting your body in any real way. The same is not true of oxygen—and it's a good thing too!

Oxygen is the life-sustaining part of Earth's atmosphere. Nearly every living thing on Earth needs oxygen to survive. Every cell in your body requires oxygen to work properly. Your body gets the oxygen it needs when you breathe air—or atmosphere—into your lungs.

Oxygen is one of Earth's 94 *naturally occurring chemical elements*—meaning a substance that can't be broken down by any natural means on Earth. While nitrogen and argon are inert gases, oxygen reacts easily with many other elements and chemicals. For example, in your body, oxygen reacts with carbon to create carbon dioxide, which leaves your body when you exhale. Oxygen is not only important because most living things breathe it in but because things on Earth need it to *combust*—or burn.

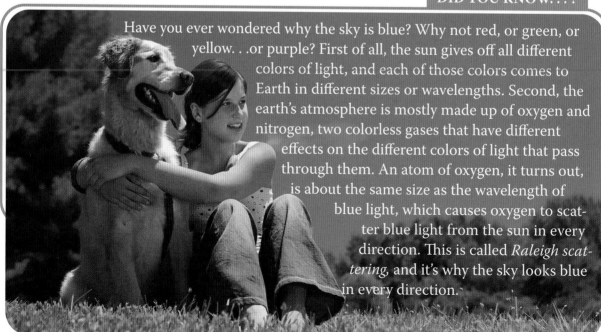

DID YOU KNOW. . .?

Have you ever wondered why the sky is blue? Why not red, or green, or yellow. . .or purple? First of all, the sun gives off all different colors of light, and each of those colors comes to Earth in different sizes or wavelengths. Second, the earth's atmosphere is mostly made up of oxygen and nitrogen, two colorless gases that have different effects on the different colors of light that pass through them. An atom of oxygen, it turns out, is about the same size as the wavelength of blue light, which causes oxygen to scatter blue light from the sun in every direction. This is called *Raleigh scattering,* and it's why the sky looks blue in every direction.

How Our Atmosphere Is Put Together

You can think of the earth's atmosphere as a thin layer of air surrounding the entire globe. The atmosphere is held in place by the earth's gravity. The higher you go above the earth's surface, the thinner the atmosphere becomes. That's because gravity pulls the atmosphere down so that it compresses on itself at lower elevations.

The main part of the earth's atmosphere is about 300 miles thick, with smaller parts of the atmosphere extending out about 6,000 miles. Most of the gases and other materials in the atmosphere are found in the first ten miles above the earth's surface.

The air pressure of our atmosphere at sea level is about 14.7 pounds per square inch, which is just about right for people and most other living things to breathe comfortably. This is called *atmospheric pressure*. But the atmosphere's air pressure decreases the higher up you go. At about 18,000 feet, the atmosphere's air pressure can be as low as half what it is at sea level.

If you've ever visited a place that is high above sea level—like on a high mountaintop or in a city like Denver, Colorado—you might have noticed that it was a little harder to breathe. That's because there is less oxygen in the air at higher altitudes, which means your lungs have to work harder to collect enough to keep you going.

The atmosphere not only keeps oxygen where humans and other life-forms need it to be, but it also acts like a blanket that insulates the earth and keeps it from becoming extremely hot or extremely cold.

BE AWARE OF THESE HIGH ALTITUDE HAZARDS:
ALTITUDE SICKNESS
REGARDLESS OF FITNESS LEVEL, "LIGHTHEADEDNESS" AND DISORIENTATION OFTEN OCCUR AT THIS ELEVATION. YOU MAY FAINT OR UNDERESTIMATE OTHER DANGERS. IF YOU EXPERIENCE ANY OF THESE SYMPTOMS AVOID PHYSICAL EXERTION AND BREATHING TOO SLOW AND TOO SHALLOW. EXERCISING CAUTION, RETURN TO A LOWER ELEVATION. IF SYMPTOMS DO NOT SUBSIDE, SEEK MEDICAL ASSISTANCE.
LIGHTNING
IF A STORM APPROACHES, TAKE SHELTER IMMEDIATELY OR CROUCH LOW WITH ONLY YOUR FEET IN CONTACT WITH THE GROUND. ONE OF THE SAFEST PLACES IS INSIDE A VEHICLE.
HYPOTHERMIA
STAY DRY, WEAR A COAT AND HAT.

This warning sign, on Colorado's Mount Evans, warns visitors of the dangers of "thin air."

41

The Layers of Our Atmosphere

In chapter 1, you read about how the earth is made up of several different layers, each of which was constructed very differently from one another. The same thing is true of the atmosphere that surrounds Earth.

The layer of the earth's atmosphere closest to the ground—the part we live in—is called the *troposphere*. Our troposphere goes up from the earth's surface about 11 miles. The troposphere is where all Earth's weather occurs, and it's also where most of the gases in our atmosphere are concentrated.

The next level of Earth's atmosphere is a thin transitional layer between the troposphere and the stratosphere called the *tropopause*. The *stratosphere* begins about 11 miles from the earth's surface and ends around 31 miles up. This is where the earth's ozone layer is found. *Ozone* is a form of oxygen that is crucial to the survival of life on Earth because it absorbs much of the sun's ultraviolet light, which is very dangerous to people and other living things if they are exposed to it in high doses.

The earth's stratosphere is followed by a layer called the *mesosphere*, which begins about 31 miles above the earth's surface and ends about 50 miles up. Next is the *ionosphere*, which starts between 43 and 45 miles up and continues out about 400 miles. The ionosphere is followed by the *exosphere*, which goes from about 400 miles out to about 800 miles above Earth's surface. The exosphere and part of the ionosphere together make up what is called the *thermosphere*.

Weather. . .an Important Function of the Atmosphere

Take a look outside right now and ask yourself what the weather is like. Is it sunny and warm? Is it cloudy and rainy? Or is it windy and cold? We use the word *weather* to describe what our atmosphere is doing around us on a given day—whether it's warm and dry, cool and rainy, clear and warm. Weather includes factors like cloudiness, *precipitation* (rain, snow, hail, and other kinds of moisture that fall from the sky), windiness, temperature, and *humidity* (how much water vapor is in the air).

Wet, cool weather can sometimes be a disappointment when you want to be outside enjoying yourself. Who wouldn't rather be outdoors on a nice sunny day than stuck inside on a rainy and cold one? But different kinds of weather serve different purposes—and all of them are important for life on Earth. For example, when it rains, water falls on the soil plants grow in and gives them the moisture they need to continue growing. And when the rain stops and the sky clears, those same plants receive an extra shot of sunlight, which is also necessary for them to grow.

Rain is produced when water evaporates and rises up to the sky, forming clouds. When the clouds start moving, the water vapor condenses, forming larger drops of water. When the drops become big and heavy enough, gravity from the earth pulls them downward. When that happens, we have rain!

Snow happens basically the same way, but with a few differences. Snow forms when the temperature in the clouds is cold enough for water vapor to condense and turn into ice. The tiny drops of moisture then start to stick together and become ice crystals. When enough of the ice crystals have gathered together, they begin to fall from the sky (again, getting some help from gravity). If the temperature between the clouds and the ground is cold enough, the ice crystals reach the ground as snowflakes. If not, they reach the ground as rain or a mixture of rain and snow called *sleet*.

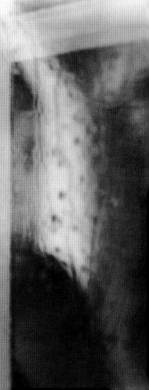

Hail also starts as droplets of water. When a strong upward wind from the surface of the earth pushes the drops above the freezing level, the droplets freeze. When they become heavy enough, they start to fall toward Earth. At that point, these balls of ice usually either melt and fall as rain or stay solid and fall as hail. Sometimes, if the upward wind is strong enough, the wind pushes the hailstones back up above the freezing level, where they become bigger hailstones.

These baseball-sized hailstones fell on Wisconsin in 2007.

THAT'S WEIRD!

Late in December 2006, a couple living in Folsom, California, reported what had to be the strangest weather event they had ever seen. It was *raining fish*! Even if the story seems a little hard to swallow, in truth there are several instances of fish falling from the sky worldwide every year. It can happen when *waterspouts*—tornadoes over water with winds as high as 200 miles per hour—suck fish out of the water and drop them over land. People as far as 100 miles inland have witnessed raining fish.

Like a tornado, a waterspout is made up of whirling winds—that suck up water from lakes or seas.

How Do Clouds Work?

Clouds are actually collections of tiny droplets of water or ice that are small enough for wind to carry them upward from the earth's surface. Most clouds form when water evaporates in the ocean or other big bodies of water, but some clouds can form over land—that is, when there is enough moisture in them.

There are four main types of clouds: cumulus, cirrus, stratus, and nimbus. When you see white, fluffy clouds in the sky—you know, the ones that can sometimes look like animals or people if you use your imagination—you're seeing *cumulus clouds*. But sometimes cumulus clouds can be thick and gray. When you see a big, gray cumulus cloud, then it will probably rain soon. Cumulus clouds are formed when warm air carries water vapor from the ground. When that warm, wet air meets cold air in the sky, the vapor condenses into droplets of water and forms a cumulus cloud.

Cirrus clouds are the thin, wispy clouds you sometimes see high in the sky—even on a very nice day. Cirrus clouds look the way they do because they are made of ice crystals instead of water droplets. Cirrus clouds form high in the sky where it is cold enough for water droplets to freeze.

Stratus clouds look like big, gray blankets hanging low in the sky. If you see stratus clouds, then you can be pretty sure that it's going to rain—or snow if it's cold enough outside. Stratus clouds can hang so low from the sky that they touch the ground. That is what we call *fog*.

When you see a *nimbus cloud* headed your way, it's probably a good idea to get inside. That's because nimbus clouds are often the source of thunderstorms—and sometimes tornadoes. Many times when you see a nimbus cloud on the horizon, you can already see that it has rain—or snow, or sometimes hail—falling out of it. You might even be able to see the flashes of lightning too!

There are a few other kinds of clouds, and most of them are combinations of the basic four listed above. There is the *cumulonimbus* cloud, which is a cumulus cloud with rain coming out of it. This cloud can be the source of some really bad weather—even tornadoes. There is also the *stratonimbus* cloud, which is a stratus cloud that looks like a gray blanket with rain falling out of it.

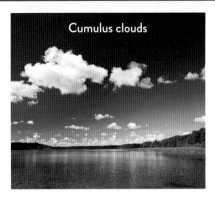

Cumulus clouds

Cirrus clouds

Stratus clouds

Nimbus clouds

What's with the Wind?

Do you like really windy days? Some people like windy days, but some don't like them at all. Some people are even afraid of really strong wind. But wind is an important part of how our earth keeps itself from overheating. That's because wind helps move heat around and equalize it, and also because it moves heat away from the earth's surface and up into the higher parts of the atmosphere.

This barometer measures changes in atmospheric pressure to predict the weather.

Wind happens when air moves from a place where the air pressure—also known as *barometric pressure*—is high to a place where the air pressure is low. How strong the wind blows depends on how big the difference in air pressure is between two places. When there are big differences in air pressure between two places, the wind will be stronger. Sometimes the differences are so great that violent storms like hurricanes and cyclones start. But when the difference isn't too great, the wind will be weaker—maybe even a nice, gentle breeze.

Several different factors can cause the differences in air pressure that result in wind. These factors include heat from the sun. Different parts of the earth receive different amounts of heat and light from the sun. This causes the temperatures to be hot near the equator and cold at the North Pole and South Pole. Extreme heat causes low pressure and extreme cold causes high pressure. That's because hot air tends to rise while cold air tends to stay close to the ground. These extreme differences in temperatures cause differences in barometric pressure, which causes wind.

If you're looking for a good illustration of how wind works, try this. Take two balloons that are about the same size. Blow one of them up until it is filled with air—don't tie it off. Blow the other balloon up halfway so that it is still soft and squishy. Now, hold each balloon at the bottom, then let them go at the same time. You'll notice that the balloon you filled completely flies around the room faster and longer than the one you filled halfway. That's because the balloon you filled completely has higher air pressure inside it, so the air comes out of it faster as the air inside the balloon tries to equalize itself with the air outside the balloon.

Climate and Weather: What's the Difference?

There are many factors that determine what kind of weather you see around you. One of those factors is the *climate* you live in. Climate isn't exactly the same thing as weather, but it has everything to do with the kind of weather you usually see where you live.

Weather is what happens in a small area of the world during a short period of time. Weather can and does change often. For example, it might be rainy and cool where you are today, but tomorrow it just might be sunny and warm. Or if it's cold and snowy this week, next week it might be warmer and rainy.

On the other hand, the *climate* of a certain part of the world is usually determined by the kind of weather that area experiences over a long period of time—usually about 30 years. The climates of different parts of the world can be dry or wet, warm or cool—and everything in between. But that doesn't mean that the area won't sometimes experience weather that doesn't exactly fit in with the climate it is known for.

Some parts of the world are known for extreme climates. For example, the Sahara Desert in northern Africa is known for very dry, very hot weather. Antarctica, which is located in the extreme southern part of planet Earth, is known for extremely cold weather—way too cold for people to live there.

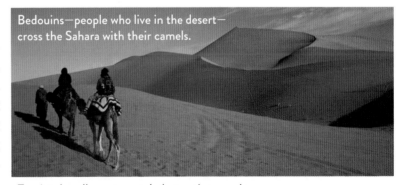
Bedouins—people who live in the desert—cross the Sahara with their camels.

Tourists bundle up to watch Antarctic penguins—who watch the people in return.

RECORD BREAKING

Here's the classic image of Death Valley—a bleached cow skull baking on dry, cracked soil.

Most of us are lucky enough not to be living in places where the temperatures get extremely hot or extremely cold. But there are places in the world where records are set. The hottest daily temperature on record took place in a place called El Azizia, Libya (Libya is a country in North Africa). Way back on September 13, 1922, the temperature there reached 136 degrees Fahrenheit. The hottest temperature ever recorded in the United States was 134 degrees Fahrenheit, recorded on July 10, 1913, in Death Valley, California. The coldest temperature ever recorded was on July 21, 1983, in Vostok Station in Antarctica (it is winter in Antarctica in July), where it reached negative 128.6 degrees Fahrenheit.

The plants in Washington's Olympic National Park like all that rain—it's one of the wettest places in the United States.

If you don't like rain, then the Atacama Desert in Chile might be the place for you. This area receives an average of about one inch of rainfall a year, but in some spots there has never been measurable rainfall recorded since people started keeping track of weather. Nothing lives in the driest parts of the Atacama Desert, not even cactus plants! On the other hand, if you like rain—*really* like rain—then you would probably like Mawsynram, a village in northeastern India, which receives around 467 inches—almost 39 feet!—of rain each year.

Things That Affect Climate

Several factors affect climate in different parts of the world. These factors include an area's distance from the equator, distance from the ocean, altitude, and distance from mountains.

The equator receives more direct sunlight than the rest of the world, so it is warmer. If you were to travel north or south from the equator, you would probably notice that the weather gets cooler and cooler the farther you get from the equator. By the time you reached the North Pole or South Pole, you'd look around you and see that everything is covered in ice and snow.

Coastal areas are usually cooler and wetter than inland areas. That is because clouds form over water when warm air collides with cool air from the sea. Areas close to large bodies of water also tend to be more humid because water from the ocean, sea, or lake evaporates. Generally, the closer you are to the ocean or sea—or other large body of water—the wetter and cooler the air will be where you live. On the other hand, the farther you live from big bodies of water, the drier it will be where you live. That's because moisture from these bodies of water evaporates before it can reach you.

Altitude, meaning how far above sea level a certain place is located, affects climate because places that are farther away from sea level receive less heat and energy from the sun. You can easily see evidence of that fact when you look at a mountain—or a picture of one, if you don't live near a mountain range. Even when the ground is dry, the mountaintop (if it is in a climate where it is possible for snow to fall) is covered in ice and snow. That's simply because it's colder up there!

That seems a little backward, doesn't it? You would think that since higher places are closer to the sun, they would be warmer. But it doesn't work that way. Actually, the atmosphere isn't warmed directly by the sun's rays. The earth's surface absorbs most of the heat from the sun, and as it warms up, it heats the atmosphere. The lower levels of the atmosphere—the ones close to the earth's surface—absorb and trap most of the heat, leaving very little of it to reach high altitudes.

Mountains can have a huge effect on the climate of the lands around them. In some coastal areas, mountains block rain from reaching inland areas. In situations like that, land on one side of the mountain may be very rainy, but the other side will be drier. In the Pacific Northwest, for example, the Coast Range and the Cascade Mountains each keep inland areas from receiving as much rain as they would have. That's why it's very rainy on the Oregon and Washington coast, less rainy in the inland parts of the states, and drier east of the Cascade Mountains.

Skiers are glad that air gets colder as you go up a mountain!

CHAPTER 4

DAY 3

THE OCEANS. . .THE LAND. . . AND THE PLANTS

Then God said, "Let the waters beneath the sky flow together into one place, so dry ground may appear." And that is what happened. God called the dry ground "land" and the waters "seas." And God saw that it was good. Then God said, "Let the land sprout with vegetation—every sort of seed-bearing plant, and trees that grow seed-bearing fruit. These seeds will then produce the kinds of plants and trees from which they came." And that is what happened. The land produced vegetation—all sorts of seed-bearing plants, and trees with seed-bearing fruit. Their seeds produced plants and trees of the same kind. And God saw that it was good. And evening passed and morning came, marking the third day.

GENESIS 1:9–13

During the first two days of creation, God laid the groundwork for a world that would look very much like it looks today. From the beginning, God intended that our earth would include oceans and land area that would serve as homes to the amazing number of plants, animals, and other living things He would create just a few days later.

On the third day of creation, God took what had been a fairly shapeless earth and turned it into one with oceans and other bodies of water separating huge pieces of land that would later be home to us humans. Not only that, He stocked the entire earth with plants—the living things that would later support all life on Earth.

Water, Water Everywhere!

Planet Earth is a one-of-a-kind creation because it is the only planet circling our sun that has oceans. In fact, no other planet known to humans has liquid water, which is necessary for supporting all known forms of life.

The oceans cover about 71 percent of the earth's surface and hold about 97 percent of all water on Earth. The Pacific Ocean is by far the biggest ocean in the world. It covers more than 64 million square miles of the earth's surface and has an average depth of about 14,000 feet. The Pacific is almost twice as big as the second largest ocean, the Atlantic. The Indian Ocean is the third biggest ocean in the world, followed by the Southern Ocean and the Arctic Ocean.

Up until the year 2000, four oceans were recognized—the Pacific, the Atlantic, the Indian, and the Arctic. That doesn't mean that the earth suddenly developed a new ocean. It means that another area of salt water was recognized as an ocean. In the spring of 2000, the International Hydrographic Organization recognized the Southern Ocean, which surrounds Antarctica deep in the Southern Hemisphere.

While there are only five oceans in the world, there are more than 85 seas. Seas are filled with salt water, just like oceans, but they are usually smaller than oceans. In fact, many seas are smaller parts of oceans. For example, the Caribbean Sea, which is located southeast of the Gulf of Mexico, is a part of the Atlantic Ocean. The Pacific Ocean has more than 30 seas. Some seas aren't part of oceans but are completely surrounded by land. These are called *landlocked seas*, and they include the Dead Sea and the Caspian Sea.

Salt collects on the shore of the Dead Sea in Israel.

Even though humans have named five different oceans, all the world's oceans are actually connected with one another through currents that flow around the world. The five named oceans are divided up according to continents and other features in the ocean, such as ridges on the ocean floor. This huge body of salt water is sometimes called the *World Ocean* or *global ocean*. The World Ocean covers about 139 million square miles of the earth's surface and has an average depth of about 12,230 feet.

THAT'S AMAZING!

The deepest water on Earth is called the Challenger Deep, a spot located in the Mariana Islands group at the southern end of the Mariana Trench in the Pacific Ocean—south of Japan, north of New Guinea, and east of the Philippines. No one knows for sure how deep the water there really is, but estimates tell us that it is more than 36,000 feet (almost seven miles) deep! Also amazing is the fact that scientists have found life on the floor of the Mariana Trench, including sea cucumbers, scale worms, shrimps, and other small organisms.

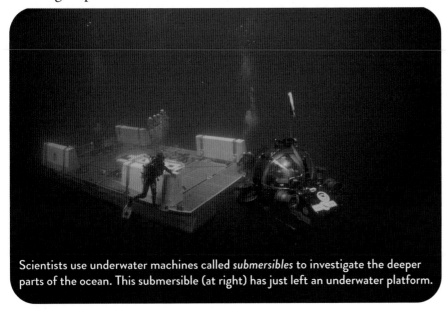

Scientists use underwater machines called *submersibles* to investigate the deeper parts of the ocean. This submersible (at right) has just left an underwater platform.

Why the Oceans Are Important to Us

Even if you don't live near an ocean, the world's oceans play a bigger part in your life than you realize. First of all, oceans are important to all life on Earth because they have a huge effect on weather and temperatures all over the world—even places that are far from any ocean.

Oceans help keep most of the surface of the earth from getting too hot or too cold because they absorb a lot of heat and light from the sun. They influence the entire world's weather by moving the warmth they absorb from the sun around the world through ocean currents and winds.

Oceans are also the source of most rain that falls on land all over the world. When water from the ocean evaporates, it leaves the salt and other materials behind and forms clouds. The clouds that form from the evaporated water then move over land, where the water in them condenses and then falls as life-giving rain.

Oceans are also important to people because they are huge sources of food such as fish, shrimps, crabs, and lobsters. Millions of people worldwide eat food that comes from the sea. That includes about 29 million tons of fish every year.

Another reason oceans are important to people is that many of the world's important goods are moved by ships that travel the ocean between the world's seaports. Those shipped goods include food, petroleum, and other important products you and your family use every day.

A fisherman pulls a net from the Atlantic Ocean, off the West African nation of Sierra Leone.

DID YOU KNOW. . . ?

Have you ever wondered why oceans and other big bodies of water have high tides and low tides every day? Believe it or not, it has to do with gravity—from the moon! The moon's gravity pulls at the water in the oceans so that they begin to bulge out in the direction of the moon. If you think that's amazing, then wait till you hear this! The water in the oceans on the side of the earth facing *away* from the moon also bulges out and forms tides. That's because Earth is being pulled toward the moon and away from the water on the opposite side of the earth. High tides and low tides happen twice each day because the earth is rotating, which means that one-half of the earth is always facing away from the moon.

The moon reflects off the Mediterranean Sea over the French Riviera.

Up until the late 1400s, many European explorers traveled to other places in Europe and to Africa, but they wouldn't sail into the Atlantic Ocean. And why not? First of all, no one had ever done it, and the explorers didn't want to risk sailing into unknown waters. But they were also afraid of the myths they heard about the Atlantic—that the water far from shore was boiling and filled with horrible sea monsters. That all changed when in 1492, Christopher Columbus and his crew sailed across the Atlantic— without seeing any boiling water or sea monsters.

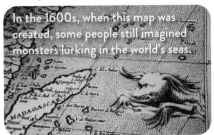
In the 1600s, when this map was created, some people still imagined monsters lurking in the world's seas.

The Ocean: A Perfect Home for Lots of Living Things

One of the reasons God created the oceans and seas was to provide a home for millions of different forms of life He would be making a few days later. To this day, the oceans are home to an amazing variety of creatures and plants that simply couldn't live anywhere else.

A big part of what makes oceans different from freshwater lakes and rivers is the saltiness of the water. Ocean water is salty because more than 30 different elements, ions, and compounds are dissolved in it. Six of those—chloride, sulfate, sodium (a scientific word for salt), magnesium, calcium, and potassium—make up about 99 percent of the total. The average saltiness of the ocean is about 35 parts per 1,000. That means that for every 1,000 ounces of seawater, 35 of those ounces are made up of "sea salt."

The chemical makeup of salt water makes it possible for the oceans and most of the seas to support countless kinds of life. Many kinds of animals and plants are designed to live in and near salt water. That includes tiny creatures called *plankton*, which are food for many other ocean creatures, all the way up to the world's biggest animal, the blue whale. Whales, seals, fish, crustaceans, jellyfish, and many other animals live in the ocean. More than 15,000 known species of fish live in the ocean, with many new kinds of saltwater fish being discovered and named every year. Also, there are more than 200,000 other animals and plants living in the world's oceans.

The Great Barrier Reef is a place where the waters "swarm with fish and other life" (Genesis 1:20).

The Great Barrier Reef, which is located off the coast of Queensland in northern Australia and stretches to a length of 1,616 miles, is such an amazing wonder of nature—and the creativity of God—that it has been called the largest living organism in the world. An amazing 4,000 species of mollusks, 1,500 species of fish (including 125 species of sharks), 400 species of corals, 215 species of birds, 500 species of seaweed, 17 species of sea snakes, and 6 species of sea turtles make their home there. Take the time to look up the Great Barrier Reef and see what kinds of animals and fish live there.

Lots of dry land—in the African nation of Namibia.

Land: The Other Part of the Earth's Surface

About 29 percent (less than one-third) of the earth's surface is dry land. This part of the world is called the *continental area*. Most of the dry land on Earth is joined together in big masses we now call *continents*. Most people recognize seven continents: North America, South America, Africa, Asia, Europe, Australia, and Antarctica. More than two-thirds of the continental area is north of the equator.

Not everyone agrees that there are seven continents on Earth. That's because some continents are joined to one another by land. Some people also believe that Europe and Asia are parts of a huge continent called *Eurasia*. Some even believe that Eurasia and Africa are one continent, which they call *Eurafrasia*. Some believe that North America and South America combined actually form one continent called the *Americas*. And some people believe that Australia is only one part of a larger continent that includes New Zealand and the Pacific Islands. They call that continent *Oceania*.

Asia is by far the largest of the seven most commonly recognized continents. Asia covers more than 17 million square miles, which is almost 30 percent of the world's total land area. Asia is the only continent that borders two other continents—Africa and Europe—which are to the west of Asia. It is bordered to the east by the Pacific Ocean.

RECORD BREAKING

Asia is not only the world's largest continent, it is also home to some other kinds of world records—namely, the highest point on Earth and the lowest point on land. The peak of Mount Everest, which is located on the border of Nepal and Tibet, is the highest place in the world at more than 29,000 feet above sea level. The lowest point on land is the Dead Sea, which is located between Israel and Jordan and sits around 1,370 feet *below* sea level.

Mount Everest, lit by the late-afternoon sun.

The Great Wall of China is one of Asia's best-known landmarks. Here it crosses mountaintops near Beijing.

The Asian continent is so big that it is divided into five subregions: Northern Asia, Middle East, Southern Asia, Eastern Asia, and Southeastern Asia. Asia is also the continent with the most people living on it. Right now, six out of ten people alive on Earth live in Asia.

Africa is known for its fascinating wildlife. Safaris—special trips for tourists—allow people to see animals up close, like these elephants in Tanzania.

Africa is the world's second biggest continent at more than 11 million square miles, or about 20 percent of the world's total land area. Africa sits on the equator and stretches about 4,970 miles from its most northern point to its most southern tip. At its widest point, Africa is about 4,700 miles wide.

Niagara Falls connects the two largest nations of North America—the United States and Canada. Notice the boat in the river below the falls!

The third largest continent is North America, which includes the United States, Canada, Mexico, and the Caribbean and Central American nations. North America is also home to Greenland, the world's largest island. North America covers more than 9.4 million square miles of the earth's surface and accounts for about 16.5 percent of the world's land.

A giant statue of Jesus—Christ the Redeemer—overlooks one of South America's most important cities, Rio de Janeiro, Brazil.

South America is the world's fourth largest continent, covering more than 6.8 million square miles and making up about 12 percent of the earth's land. South America is home to some amazing natural wonders, including the Amazon River, which is more than 3,900 miles long—the second longest river on the planet—as well as the largest tropical rain forest in the world. The Andes Mountains stretch the entire length of the continent.

Antarctica, which is the fifth largest continent by area, accounts for around 9.2 percent of the earth's land mass. Antarctica is almost completely covered year-round by a thick layer of ice. It is the coldest place on Earth, with temperatures in some parts of the continent sometimes dipping all the way down to below negative 100 degrees Fahrenheit! That's why Antarctica is last in total population. No one lives in Antarctica permanently, but a few thousand scientists work there during the summer, with only around a thousand of them staying through the winter.

Europe is the world's second smallest continent by area, covering just over 3.9 million square miles, or about 6.8 percent of the world's land mass.

Australia is the smallest continent by area, accounting for about 5.9 percent of the world's land.

Ice, snow, and penguins are among the main features of Antarctica. What you won't find are many people!

The Eiffel Tower in Paris, France, is one of Europe's best-known landmarks. It was built in the late 1880s for a world's fair.

Ayers Rock, also called Uluru, is one of Australia's most famous natural landmarks. It's nearly six miles around—that's a big rock!

Where Do Continents End and the Oceans Begin?

Nearly all continents are surrounded from their beaches out toward the ocean by an extension of underwater land in the shallow part of the oceans called the *continental shelf*. The water over the continental shelf is usually not more than 500 to 650 feet deep. How wide a continental shelf is depends on the continent and its geological features. Some areas have almost no continental shelf, while some have continental shelves wider than 250 miles. For areas that do have continental shelves, the average shelf is about 50 miles in width. The largest continental shelf is called the Serbian Shelf. It is located in the Arctic Ocean and stretches 930 miles from shore.

The continental shelf is actually made up of several parts. The first part of the continental shelf starts just outside the shoreline of the continent. As you move from the shoreline out into the deeper parts of the ocean, the shelf slopes smoothly until it reaches what is called the *continental shelf break*. The continental shelf break usually starts in ocean waters about 430 feet deep. After the continental break, the floor of the ocean turns quickly downward. This feature of geology is called the *continental slope*. Farther out from the continental slope is the *continental rise*, which is a deposit of sediments that form as a result of runoff from the continent's streams and rivers. After the continental rise is what geologists call the *abyssal plains*, which is a scientific way of saying the deepest parts of the ocean.

The continental shelf isn't always flat. Some parts of the continental shelf include deep valleys as well as tall mountains and hills. Some of these mountains reach up past the surface of the sea, creating islands. Islands that stand on a continent's continental shelf are considered part of that continent.

The continental shelf is home to most of the kinds of plants and animals that live in the ocean—including fish and other living things that humans harvest and eat. This part of the ocean supports the most kinds of life because it receives more sunlight and because the sediment that washes into the ocean from the continent's rivers and streams provides nourishment for microscopic plants and animals that larger animals, such as fish, feed on. The continental shelf also supports the largest amounts of plants and animals that live on the ocean floor.

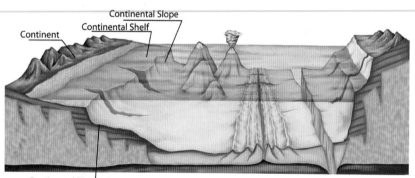

The continental shelf is a shallow underwater plain that makes up a continent's true outer edge. It can be a few miles to more than 200 miles wide, before dropping off quickly to the deep ocean floor.

Islands Big and Small

It might surprise you to hear this, but today one out of every ten people living in the world live on islands. But when you realize that 200 million people live in Indonesia—which is made up entirely of islands—and that more than 60 million live on the island of Great Britain, it's not hard to imagine how so many people live on islands today.

Islands are bodies of land that are surrounded on all sides by water. Continents are also surrounded by water, but they are much larger and are therefore classified as continents. For example, Australia is surrounded by water, but it covers almost three million square miles. That's why Australia is considered a continent. Greenland, which is the world's largest island, is about one-fourth the size of Australia and is therefore considered an island.

It's hard to say how many islands there are in the world. Today people live on more than 100,000 of the world's islands, and there are many times more islands that people don't live on. The Asian island nation of Indonesia leads the world with a total of 13,667 islands, 6,000 of which are inhabited by people.

There are many kinds of islands in the world. Islands that sit on the continental shelf of a certain continent are called *continental islands*. The nations of Great Britain, Ireland, New Guinea, Barbados, and several others are all considered continental islands. Islands that sit in the ocean away from a continental shelf are called *oceanic islands*. Scientists believe that almost all oceanic islands were made as the result of volcanoes. The Hawaiian Islands are examples of volcanic islands.

The smallest island in the world is Bishop Rock, which is located at the southwestern part of the United Kingdom. Actually, Bishop Rock is little more than that: a rock, sticking up out of the water. Greenland, on the other hand, covers about 840,000 square miles.

Bishop Rock island is just big enough to hold this lighthouse!

Red-hot lava bursts out of a volcano called Piton de la Fournaise, on the Indian Ocean island of Réunion.

Here's some good trivia to remember: The second tallest mountain in the world is called K2, or Mount Godwin-Austen. It's near the border of Pakistan and China.

RECORD BREAKING

You probably already know that Mount Everest, which is located in the Himalayas at the border of Tibet and Nepal, is the highest mountain peak in the world. The peak of Everest is an amazing 29,028 feet above sea level. But it might surprise you to know that Everest is not really the world's tallest mountain. That honor goes to Mauna Kea, a dormant volcano in Hawaii. Mauna Kea's peak is 13,796 feet above sea level, less than half the elevation of Everest. But if you measured from the base of Mauna Kea, which is deep on the ocean floor, you'd find it is more than 32,800 feet tall, far taller than Everest.

Observatories—buildings that house large telescopes—sit atop Hawaii's Mauna Kea. It's one of the best places in the world to see the stars.

All Land on Earth Is Not Equal

When God created the earth, then separated the water from the land, He designed many types of land masses. That includes mountain ranges, forests, deserts, valleys, canyons, plains, and other kinds of land we see on Earth today.

Some of the most amazing formations of land in the world are mountains. There are many mountains and mountain ranges on the earth. Geologists say that about 25 percent of the earth's surface is mountainous. Asia is the capital continent for mountains. More than half of Asia is covered in mountains, and all of the world's 50 tallest mountains are located there. Mountains are important to people, animals, and plants because they serve as barriers to weather and because they collect snow in the winter, which runs off the mountain when the weather warms and provides people with fresh water.

There are several kinds of mountains on Earth today. Some mountains were formed when huge plates on the earth's surface pushed against one another and caused the mountains to arise. The Rocky Mountains in North America are examples of those kinds of mountains. Other mountains were formed as the result of molten rock, or *magma*, pushing up from under the earth's crust. Sometimes the magma erupts and piles up on the surface, making what

Giant farm machines called *combines* harvest wheat on the plains.

is called a *volcanic mountain*. Mount Saint Helens in Washington State is a volcanic mountain.

Some areas of land on Earth have no hills or mountains and receive enough precipitation to make them suitable for farming. These areas are called *plains*. The Great Plains of North America, which are located west of the Mississippi River and east of the Rocky Mountains, produce about 25 percent of the world's wheat, oats, barley, rye, sorghum, and corn.

Some areas of the world receive enough rain and snow each year to support large numbers of plants and other life. But other areas are so dry that only certain kinds of plants and animals can live there. *Deserts* are usually defined as areas of land that receive less than ten inches of rain or snow every year.

Camels can go a long time between drinks of water—which allows them to live in desert areas. These camels are walking across China's Gobi Desert.

When God Made the World Come Alive

Imagine if someone set up a terrarium at school one day. He'd add the rocks, the sand, the water—maybe even some natural-looking decorations. Now, what do you think is missing? That's right! Plants and animals! No terrarium is complete without living things, even if they're just plants.

Creation wasn't complete until God began adding the living things He prepared Earth for in the first place. He had already finished making planet Earth a suitable home for all animals and other living things, so now it was time to begin the process of giving the earth life by filling it with every kind of living thing you can imagine—and some you can't.

The first living things God created were ones that don't move—at least not on their own: plants.

Plants live and grow just about anywhere there is sunlight and water. Plants can be found on land, in oceans, and in fresh water. Not all plants need the same amount of sunlight and water to live and grow. But God designed each and every one of them to be able to live and grow and reproduce in the different kinds of surroundings He placed them in.

There are many different types of plants living on Earth today. There are many kinds each of trees, grasses, flowers, bushes, herbs, ferns, mosses, vines, and some kinds of algae. Scientists estimate that there are about 350,000 species of plants living on Earth today, but so far almost 288,000 kinds of plants have been identified and named.

The arrival of land animals on Earth wouldn't begin for another few days. But in the meantime, God created living things that were like animals in some ways but very different in others. Plants are different from animals in three important ways.

First, plants have chlorophyll in them. *Chlorophyll* is what makes plants green and also allows them to produce their own food by absorbing sunlight. Second, the cell walls of all plants are made of a very sturdy material called *cellulose*. The cells of animals, on the other hand, don't have rigid walls the way plants do. Third, plants don't move on their own. Sure, they may seem to move as they respond to sunlight—like when a sunflower points toward the sun so that it can absorb more sunlight—but no plant can just get up and move on its own.

Why the Earth Needs Plants

Have you ever stopped and thought about how important plants are to all life on Earth? They're probably more important than you realize. First of all, plants are necessary for food for all animals—even the ones that eat mostly meat. Nearly every living creature that lives on Earth depends on plants to survive. All animals either eat plants or eat other animals that eat plants.

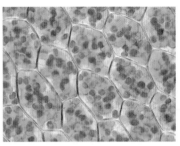

Chloroplasts, the parts of a plant cell that carry on photosynthesis, show up as green circles in this highly magnified picture.

The ability of plants to produce food is an amazing part of God's design for life on Earth. When He made plants, He gave them the ability to collect energy directly from the sun. In a process called *photosynthesis*, almost all plants use the chlorophyll stored in their leaves to convert the energy they collect from the sun into food. The plants store this energy in the form of natural sugar or *carbohydrates*—which are the basis of all food that animals and people eat. That means there are no naturally produced foods that aren't somehow based on plants.

Plants supply the earth with much more than food. During the process of photosynthesis, plants also absorb carbon dioxide and then release oxygen into the atmosphere. Scientists estimate that plants—from microscopic ones that live in the ocean to the biggest trees growing on land—produce as much as 98 percent of the breathable oxygen in the earth's atmosphere.

All this means that without plants, there would be no life on Earth—at least as we know it today. It also means that God, who created all the earth and everything that lives in it, thought ahead enough to provide all living things with all they needed to live and grow and reproduce here on Earth.

Would you eat a fungus? If you like mushrooms, you would!

If you've ever been in the produce department at your local supermarket, you've probably noticed that mushrooms are placed in the produce department—along with fruits and vegetables, all of which come from different kinds of plants. But mushrooms aren't plants and don't come from plants. They belong in what is called the fungus kingdom—along with spores and molds. That's right! Mushrooms aren't vegetables, even though your grocer puts them in the same department as fruits and vegetables. They are a part of the same kingdom of living things as molds and fungi (the plural of *fungus*).

The First Kingdom on Earth: The Plant Kingdom

By the time God was finished creating all the living things on Earth, there were millions and millions of species of plants, animals, and other life-forms. Since then, *biologists*—scientists who study living things—have sorted and classified all living things by how they are different and how they are alike.

The largest classes of living things are called *kingdoms*. All living things are classified into one of five different kingdoms, and all plants are placed in the plant kingdom (or, as some people call it, *Kingdom Plantae*).

Biologists have broken down the plant kingdom into smaller and smaller divisions based on different things that are true about different kinds of plants. The two largest divisions are between plants that can circulate water and other liquids through their roots, stems, and leaves, and plants that need to absorb all their water from their surroundings.

Spores of a mossy plant

Most plants can circulate water through their roots, stems, and leaves. Biologists call these *vascular* plants. These types of plants are then broken down by how they reproduce. Most plants reproduce through seeds, but some reproduce through spores. Plants that reproduce through seeds are called *spermatophytes*. Plants that reproduce through spores are called *pteridophytes*, and they include some mosses and ferns.

Pinecone

Some plants reproduce through seeds that aren't encased in anything. These plants are called *gymnosperms*. Many of these types of plants are very important to humans because they are a source of wood. That includes different species of cedars, firs, pines, spruces, redwoods, and others. These plants reproduce through seeds, but the seeds are stored in female cones until they are fertilized by the pollen of male cones. After the seeds mature, they are dropped out onto the ground, where they sprout and eventually mature into a fully grown plant.

Apple, showing seed inside

Most plants reproduce through seeds that are encased in things people and animals eat. You know how apples, cucumbers, pears, and other types of fruits and vegetables have seeds inside them? That's so they can reproduce and make more of their own kind. These kinds of plants are called *flowering plants*, or, more scientifically, *angiosperms*.

More Reasons to Like Plants with Flowers

Can you remember the last time you saw a beautiful flower? How about the last time you enjoyed a fresh piece of fruit or a juicy, sweet piece of corn on the cob? How about the last time you wore something made of cotton? If you can remember the last time you did one of those things, then you can remember the last time you benefited from a group of plants that scientists call the *angiosperms*.

All these types of plants have one thing in common: flowers.

Not all flowers are as colorful or showy as a rose or a daffodil or even a daisy. Many flowers are very small and not all that colorful. Sometimes you wouldn't even think of them as flowers. For example, oak trees, grass, and wheat plants all have flowers, but they aren't much to look at, so you don't really notice them. But all flowers, even the ones that aren't as pretty as others, serve the same purpose: reproduction of the plant.

When you hear the word *flowering*, you probably think of pretty flowers like roses, pansies, daisies, and other kinds of popular flowers. But did you know that most of our food comes from flowering plants? All grains, beans, nuts, fruits, vegetables, and spices come to our dinner tables as a result of the reproduction process of flowering plants. So do drinks like coffee, tea, and cola. Flowering plants also help us in the production of a lot of our clothes. Cotton and linen are produced from the fibers of flowering plants. A lot of the medicines we use are also made from flowering plants.

The plant world includes some of the strangest of all God's created things. Did you know that there are plants that eat meat? It's true! Instead of taking all their nourishment through their roots and from sunlight, like most plants do, these plants trap and eat insects and sometimes (are you ready for this?) small amphibians, reptiles, birds, and mammals. Probably the best known of   the carnivorous plants is the Venus flytrap. But there are several other plants that eat meat. They include bladderworts, butterworts, pitcher plants, sundews, and cobra lilies.

Look out, fly—you're about to become lunch!

Flowering plants reproduce through a process called *pollination.* Pollination happens when male plant spores (the pollen) combine with the female reproductive cells. Once pollination takes place, the plant begins to produce seeds and fruit. Pollen from a flowering plant is dusty-looking stuff that is most often yellow but can also be black, white, green, orange, or just about any other color you can think of.

Different kinds of flowering plants pollinate in different ways. Some plants need the help of birds and bats as well as bees and other insects to pollinate. Other kinds of plants are pollinated when the wind picks up their pollen and spreads it out onto other plants of the same species. A few plants, such as peanut plants, just pollinate themselves.

Pollination is a necessary part of a flowering plant's life cycle. Without pollination, flowering plants can't reproduce. That means they couldn't bear fruit or seeds. If pollination were to suddenly stop, then almost all the earth's plant life would soon begin to die off.

CHAPTER 5

DAY 4
SOME GREAT STUFF GOD MADE "OUT THERE"

Then God said, "Let lights appear in the sky to separate the day from the night. Let them be signs to mark the seasons, days, and years. Let these lights in the sky shine down on the earth." And that is what happened. God made two great lights—the larger one to govern the day, and the smaller one to govern the night. He also made the stars. God set these lights in the sky to light the earth, to govern the day and night, and to separate the light from the darkness. And God saw that it was good. And evening passed and morning came, marking the fourth day.

Genesis 1:14–19

SOME GREAT STUFF GOD MADE "OUT THERE"

On the fourth day of creation, God made things that have amazed and confused humans since the beginning of time. On that day, He made the things that aren't really part of the planet Earth but that are still important parts of His creation. That includes the objects we can easily see in the sky, like the sun, the moon, and some of the stars and planets. But it also includes things in outer space that it took thousands of years for people to figure out how to see from here on Earth. All of these things that God made and placed out in space on the fourth day of creation make up what we now call the *universe*.

When you start to understand some things about what God really did on the fourth day of creation, you'll be amazed. But you'll also begin to understand that even though our planet is very, very big, it is really just a tiny speck in an unbelievably huge universe.

One of the great things about knowing a little something about the stars, planets, galaxies, and other things God made on that fourth day of creation is that it helps you to understand just how big and awesome the God who made all those things really is!

Giant radio antennas in California's Mojave Desert scan the skies, helping scientists learn more about the gigantic universe we live in.

Just How Big Is the Universe Anyway?

Almost since we first noticed the sun, the moon, the stars, and other mysterious objects in the sky, we humans have tried our best to discover what's out there in that enormous universe God created.

Thousands of years ago, people started to get the fact that the universe God created was really big and really amazing and that it included some amazing creations. But it wasn't until the past several hundred years that we started to understand just *how* big it really is.

No one knows for sure how big the universe is. So far, *astronomers*—scientists who study things in outer space—have located objects as far away from Earth as 10 to 13 billion light-years (for a quick reminder of how far a light-year is, look back at page 15 in chapter 1). Some of these objects are called *quasars*. Scientists believe quasars are formed when two *galaxies* (huge collections of stars, which you'll read about later in this chapter) collide with one another. They believe quasars are probably huge points of light that are fueled by enormous black holes in outer space.

How many miles are in a light-year? Let's see. . .

Light travels 186,000 miles a second. . .
There are (x) 60 seconds in a minute. . .
There are (x) 60 minutes in an hour. . .
There are (x) 24 hours in a day. . .
There are (x) 365 days in a year. . .

So light travels about

5,865,696,000,000 miles in a year!

What Stars Are and How They Work

If you've ever been on a camping trip or just been outside during a really dark, clear night, you have probably seen thousands of stars in the sky. But during the day you can see the most important star to us humans: the sun! The stars you see at night look very tiny from Earth, but they are all actually huge balls of burning gas—just like our sun.

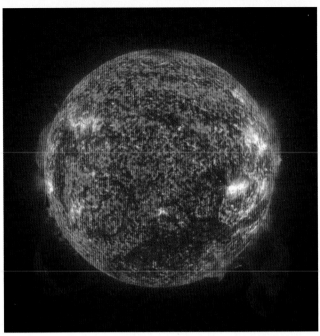

Our sun—photographed by the Solar and Heliospheric Observatory spacecraft—shoots out flares on two sides. Doesn't that look hot?

Even though stars give off huge amounts of heat and light, they don't burn the same way things burn here on Earth. For a fire to start here on Earth, you need three things: fuel, oxygen, and something to ignite the fire. Stars have plenty of fuel in the form of hydrogen, but since there is no oxygen inside stars, they have to burn another way. That way is called *nuclear fusion*, and it happens in stars when gravity from inside the star—which is many, many times as strong as the earth's gravity—pulls hydrogen inward and causes four atoms of hydrogen to fuse together to form one atom of helium. When that happens, part of the mass from the hydrogen atom is left over, and that extra mass is converted into heat and light.

Even though all stars look pretty much the same when you look at them from Earth, there are actually several kinds of stars. Some stars are very small, at least compared to other stars, and some stars are many times bigger than our sun. The smallest stars in the universe are called *neutron stars*. These are actually dead stars that are no wider than a city. The biggest stars in the universe—in fact, the biggest objects of any kind in the universe—are called *supergiant* stars. Some supergiants are more than 1,000 times bigger than our sun.

Most stars fit into a class astronomers call *main sequence stars*. Our sun is a main sequence star. Main sequence stars come in many different sizes, and many of them burn a lot brighter than others. But like our sun, all main sequence stars convert hydrogen into helium in their cores and release amazing amounts of heat and light.

RECORD BREAKING

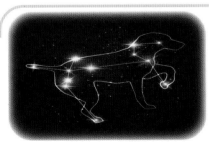

Sirius is often called the Dog Star because it's part of the "big dog" (Canis Majoris) constellation.

The biggest star known to humans is called VY Canis Majoris. It is located in the constellation Canis Majoris, which also includes Sirius, the brightest star in the sky. Scientists estimate that VY Canis Majoris is up to 2,100 times the diameter of our sun and that if it were to replace our sun, it would stretch all the way out to Saturn, the sixth planet in our solar system. VY Canis Majoris is so big that if you could hollow it out, it could hold seven billion stars the size of our sun inside it.

Constellations: Random Puzzles in the Sky

From Earth, some of the stars in the sky are grouped in a way that makes them look like connect-the-dots puzzles of animals, people, and other things. These are called *constellations*.

There are 88 named constellations. You've probably seen the Big Dipper, the Little Dipper, and other easy-to-find constellations. What constellations you see at night depends on where you live and what time of the year you look. The ones you can see in the Northern Hemisphere are different from the ones you can see in the south. For example, people in the north can see the Big Dipper and people in the south can see the Southern Cross.

Even today, some people believe that where the constellations appear in the sky affects life here on Earth. But in truth, constellations are nothing more than imaginary formations of stars in the sky. Even though the constellations may *look* like pictures of animals, people, or other things, most of them are made up of stars that are many light-years apart in space. One exception to that rule is the Big Dipper. The Big Dipper is made up of stars that really *are* close together—at least when you compare the distance between them with the distances between other stars.

People in North America call this constellation the Big Dipper—but in England, they're more likely to call it the Plough.

Here is an artist's idea of how a black hole can swallow a star: The star (left) comes within the black hole's extreme gravity and begins to break apart (center), finally swirling into the dark void (right).

Have you ever heard of a black hole? It's an object in space with such strong gravity coming from it that nothing, including light, can escape from it. Scientists believe that black holes are created when massive stars run out of fuel and die. When that happens, the star's gravity pulls its material inward and compresses its core, which creates a supernova explosion. What is left over after the explosion is the star's core. The core's gravitational pull is so strong that not even light can escape it. The object is now a black hole. Although scientists can't really see black holes, they can find them by watching how objects around them are affected.

What Happens When a Really Big Star Dies? A Supernova!

All stars have a certain amount of fuel they can burn to produce light and heat. When the fuel in a really big star runs out, that star begins to die. When that happens, the star explodes and forms what astronomers call a *supernova*. A supernova is a gigantic explosion that makes the star brighter than all the other stars.

When the supernova is finished, what is left is a huge cloud called a *nebula* and a compressed star called a *neutron star*. If the star that exploded is one of the biggest stars in the universe, then it leaves behind a nebula or what is called a *black hole*.

Supernovas are very rare events. But every year astronomers see about 300 supernovas in other galaxies. Almost a thousand years ago, astronomers in China, Japan, Korea, and Arabia recorded a supernova that was so bright it could be seen during the day. That supernova formed what is now known as the Crab Nebula.

See the bright star to the lower left of the spiral galaxy? That's a supernova—brighter than other stars because it's in the process of exploding!

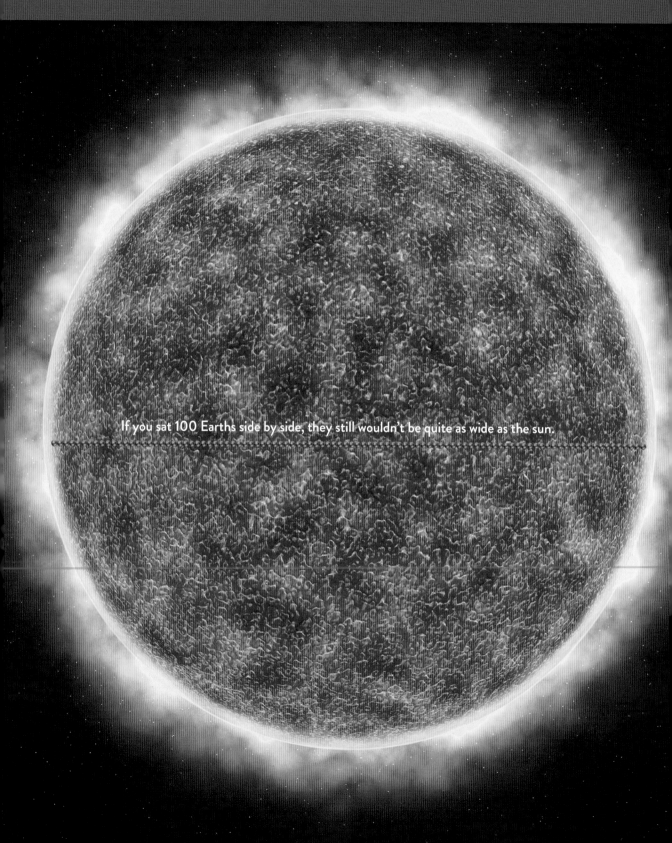

If you sat 100 Earths side by side, they still wouldn't be quite as wide as the sun.

Earth's Own Star: The Sun

When you see the sun, you're actually seeing a medium-sized star. The sun is made up of about three-quarters hydrogen and one-quarter helium. The sun's gravity holds planets and other objects in our solar system and keeps them orbiting around it.

The earth gets all its heat and light from the sun. Without that heat and light, plants and animals and people couldn't live on Earth. Our planet can support the different forms of life that live here because it is the perfect distance—about 93 million miles—from the sun. If it were too much closer, the earth would be too hot to live on. If it were any farther away, it would be too cold to live here.

Maybe you haven't given much thought to the sun other than how much you like it when it shines when you're outside. But here are some facts about the sun that just might amaze you. The temperature on the sun's surface is about 10,000 degrees Fahrenheit. Think that's hot? Try this: the temperature deep *inside* the sun is about 27 *million* degrees. The sun is about 870,000 miles wide—about 109 times wider than the earth.

Why We Have Seasons

Have you ever wondered why it's cold in the winter and hot in the summer? Or why the days get longer in the spring, then start getting shorter in the fall? The sun always gives off about the same amount of heat and light, so it can't be that someone just turns down the heat every winter.

Here's how it *really* works.

The earth travels all the way around the sun about once every 365 days. But it doesn't orbit the sun with the same spots on the planet pointing directly at the sun all the time. Earth leans to one side as it orbits the sun, so different parts of the earth point more directly at the sun than others during different times of the year. This means that different amounts of sunlight reach different points on the earth during different times of the year. The different amounts of sunlight cause different kinds of weather during those different times. In other words, it's colder when where you live on Earth is farthest from the sun and hotter when it's the closest.

During the summer in the Northern Hemisphere, that part of the earth is pointed more directly at the sun, so it receives more heat and light from the sun than it does in the winter. At that same time, the Southern Hemisphere is *farthest* away from the sun, so it receives less of the sun's heat and light. That means that when it's summer in the Northern Hemisphere, it's winter in the Southern Hemisphere.

Astronomers Call It a Satellite. . . . We Call It the Moon

The earth is one of eight planets that orbit the sun. Most of those planets have what scientists call *satellites* orbiting them. Our earth has a satellite of its own—one you can see in the sky most nights. You know this satellite better as the *moon*.

Even though the moon looks small from the earth, it is actually very large. The moon is about 2,160 miles across, which is about one-fourth the size of Earth. It only looks small because it is about 238,900 miles from Earth. Just as the sun's gravity holds the earth and other planets orbiting in place, Earth's gravity keeps the moon in place and orbiting the earth.

A few people have walked on the moon, but the moon can't support the kinds of plants and animals—or people—that live on Earth. That's because the moon has no air on it. The moon has no air on it because the gravity there is about one-sixth what it is on Earth. That's not even enough gravity for the moon to hold an atmosphere! Also, because the moon has no atmosphere to block out the sun's light or to help it trap heat, temperatures on the moon's surface range from up to 253 degrees Fahrenheit during the day, all the way down to negative 387 degrees Fahrenheit at night.

Even though the moon is the brightest object in the nighttime sky, it doesn't give off its own light. When you see the moon shining brightly, it's because the moon is reflecting light from the sun back to Earth. The moon orbits the earth, and it spins on its axis in about the same time it takes to orbit the earth. That's why we always see the same half of the moon's surface from Earth. The other half of the moon is called the "far side" of the moon. Some people have called that side of the moon the "dark side," but that isn't correct, because the sun does shine on the side that is facing away from Earth.

Sometimes the moon looks like a big, shiny circle in the sky. But sometimes it is shaped like a crescent. At other times it looks like a sliver of light in the sky. That is because the moon shines on Earth in what are called *lunar phases*. It takes the moon about 29.5 days to complete the cycle of lunar phases and 27.3 days to orbit the earth. The moon looks different during its lunar phases because light from the sun is shining on it at different angles—at least as we see it from Earth. When the moon is full, it's because the sun is shining on the entire surface that we on Earth can see.

Only 12 humans have ever visited the moon, all of them from the United States: Neil Armstrong (the first to step onto the moon's surface), Buzz Aldrin, Charles "Pete" Conrad Jr., Alan Bean, Alan Shepard Jr., Edgar Mitchell, David Scott, James Irwin, John Young, Charles Duke Jr., Eugene Cernan, and Harrison Schmitt.

Our solar system. From right to left: the sun, Mercury, Venus, Earth, Mars, Jupiter, Saturn, Uranus, Neptune, and Pluto. This picture only shows the order of the planets—it's not to scale. The planets are much farther away from each other, and the sun is much, much larger than shown here.

Our Solar System: The Place Our Sun Calls Home

Our earth is part of a *solar system*. A solar system is made up of a star that has planets and other things orbiting around it. Our solar system includes the sun, a total of eight planets, some *dwarf planets* (more about them later), and other objects such as *comets* and *asteroids*.

Many astronomers believe that our solar system may be only one of many billions placed in the Milky Way galaxy, the galaxy our solar system is located in, alone. There are more stars in the universe than we can actually count, and astronomers believe that if even a small fraction of those stars are centers of solar systems, then there could be countless hundreds of billions of solar systems in the entire universe.

Our sun is the center of our solar system. But it's a lot more than that. The sun is far bigger and heavier than the rest of the bodies in our solar system combined. The sun actually accounts for 99.9 percent of all the mass in our solar system. That means that if you put a value of $1,000 on all the material in our solar system, the sun would be worth $999, with all the rest of the material worth one buck!

THE WAY IT USED TO BE

Galileo Galilei
(1564–1642)

Hundreds of years ago, people really believed that the earth was the center of the universe. That means they believed that the sun, the moon, the stars, and the other planets revolved around the planet we live on. That began to change when astronomers like Galileo and Nicolaus Copernicus began watching the rotations of the movement of the planets. It took awhile, but in time people came to accept the fact that the earth revolved around the sun, not the other way around.

Nicolaus Copernicus
(1473–1543)

Our Neighbors in the Solar System

The eight planets in our solar system are the biggest objects orbiting our sun. Those eight planets—from the closest to the sun to the farthest away—are Mercury, Venus, Earth, Mars, Jupiter, Saturn, Uranus, and Neptune.

Up until 2006, scientists believed there were nine planets in our solar system because they had classified Pluto as a planet. Pluto is still out there just like it always has been, but scientists have now placed it in a new class of objects in the solar system called *dwarf planets.* Dwarf planets are a lot like planets. They are sphere-shaped (like a basketball), and they orbit the sun. Some astronomers hold that dwarf planets are different from planets in that they orbit in areas of the solar system where there are many other objects also orbiting.

Water ice

Core
(iron-nickel alloy, rock)

PLUTO

Scientists believe Pluto is mainly frozen methane, with a small center of metal and rock. Far from the sun, Pluto is very, very cold—hundreds of degrees below zero.

Mercury is the smallest planet in our solar system. It is only a little bigger than our moon. Venus is sometimes called Earth's Twin Sister because it is almost the same size as Earth. Mars is a little over half the size of Earth. Uranus is about four times bigger than Earth. Saturn is the second biggest planet in the solar system. At about 75,000 miles in diameter, it is about ten times wider than Earth. Jupiter is the largest planet in our solar system. Jupiter's diameter is about 11 times the diameter of Earth. Scientists estimate that Jupiter is so big that about 1,000 planets the size of Earth could fit inside a hollowed-out Jupiter.

Listed from the smallest to the largest, our solar system's planets are Mercury, Mars, Venus, Earth, Neptune, Uranus, Saturn, and Jupiter.

Earth is the only planet that can support life as we know it. First of all, other planets are either too hot (like Mercury and Venus) or too cold (like Mars) for humans or other forms of life on Earth to live on. Second, there's no air—at least the kind we have here on Earth—or liquid water on the other planets. And never mind the fact that Jupiter and Saturn are made mostly of gases we can't breathe!

THAT'S WEIRD!

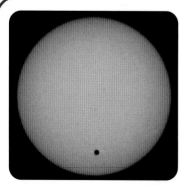

Venus, the second closest planet to the sun in our solar system, spins in the opposite direction compared to the earth and most other planets. Because of that, the sun rises in the west and sets in the east on Venus. But even if you could live on Venus, you wouldn't see the sunrise or sunset very often. That's because one day on Venus is equal to about 243 Earth days.

What's that black spot on the sun? It's the planet Venus, passing between the sun and the earth. This rare event, called a *Venus transit,* was photographed in 2004.

More Cool Stuff in Our Solar System

Planets and dwarf planets are not the only objects that orbit our sun. There are also some really amazing objects out there that fit into their own classifications. That includes asteroids and comets.

Asteroids are a lot like planets, only smaller. Asteroids orbit the sun like planets do, and they can't make their own light. Most asteroids are made out of rock, but some are made out of metal.

There are tens of thousands of known asteroids in our solar system, with thousands of new ones being discovered every month. Most of the known asteroids orbit the sun between the orbits of Mars and Jupiter in what is called the *main asteroid belt.*

Astronomers believe there are between one million and two million asteroids bigger than half a mile across in the main asteroid belt and millions of smaller ones. A few asteroids are more than 300 miles wide! At 605 miles wide, Ceres (which was also classified as a dwarf planet in 2006) is the biggest object in the asteroid belt.

Halley's Comet streaks through space at 103,000 miles an hour in this photograph from 1986. The "tail" you can see behind the comet is about 450,000 miles long.

While asteroids are made of rock and metal, *comets* are dirty, dusty balls of ice. That is why they are often called *dirty snowballs.* Many comets orbit the sun differently than the planets and asteroids. Some comets orbit from outside the solar system, then into the solar system, and then back out into outer space.

The word *comet* comes from a Greek word meaning "long-haired." Comets got that name because when they have long tails they are visible from Earth. Comets grow tails when they move close to the sun, where solar heat causes the frozen gases and dust to partially melt and form a long trail of vaporized gas, dust, and rocks.

The most famous comet is Halley's Comet, which can be seen from Earth once every 76 years as it passes close to the sun. But a comet called Shoemaker-Levy 9 became famous in July 1994 when 20 fragments of the comet crashed into the planet Jupiter.

THE WAY IT USED TO BE

People throughout history have seen bright comets in the night sky, and they believed that when they saw them it meant bad things were going to happen. They believed comets actually entered the earth's atmosphere, and they blamed wars, famines, and death on them. Some people wouldn't even leave their homes when there was a comet overhead! We now know that comets aren't signs of anything good or bad—just another part of God's creation.

In an ancient tapestry, astrologers predict trouble for England's King Harold II because of the appearance of a comet (top right) during his reign. Harold was king of England from 1022 to 1066.

The Milky Way Galaxy: A Good Home for a Solar System

This galaxy—called NGC 7331—probably looks very much like our own Milky Way galaxy. The photo was taken by the Spitzer Space Telescope.

The sun at the center of our solar system is just one of literally billions of stars God placed in what is called the *Milky Way galaxy*. The Milky Way galaxy is more than 100,000 light-years across and is home to between 100 and 400 billion stars.

A *galaxy* is a huge gathering of stars and other objects organized into a certain shape. Up until the 1920s, the Milky Way was the only known galaxy in the universe. But in 1924 an American astronomer named Edwin Hubble proved that there were several other distant galaxies in space. Since then we have learned that there are hundreds of billions of galaxies in the universe. Most galaxies are tens of thousands of light-years across and contain billions of stars.

Galaxies come in many different shapes and sizes. The Milky Way galaxy is what is called a *spiral galaxy*. Spiral galaxies are shaped like giant spinning wheels with a *hub* (a center that all the stars spin around), and curved *arms* sticking out from the center. The arms of the spiral galaxy are actually tight groups of stars. There are several types of spiral galaxies, and they are classified by the tightness of their arms.

Elliptical galaxies are egg-shaped collections of stars. These are the biggest galaxies—as large as 18 million light-years across. The third kind of galaxy, an *irregular galaxy*, has an unusual shape, so it can't be put in other groups.

Galaxies spin on their hubs at amazing speeds. That includes the Milky Way. In fact, the sun and all the planets and other objects in our solar system are zipping around the center of the Milky Way at around 150 miles per second. And if that seems fast, think about this: our entire galaxy is traveling through space at about one million miles per hour!

EXPLORING THE HEAVENS

Even if you don't own a telescope or live near a planetarium, you can still learn about some of the wonders of God's creation as they appear in space. It's as easy as stepping outside, looking up, and writing down what you see! Try this: Check out a book on astronomy at the library and look up the names of the constellations (there are 88 of them), and see what they look like and which stars are in them. After you've done that, step out your front door, look up, and see how many of them you can find in the night sky.

CHAPTER 6

DAY 5
THINGS WITH FINS,
THINGS WITH FEATHERS

Then God said, "Let the waters swarm with fish and other life. Let the skies be filled with birds of every kind." So God created great sea creatures and every living thing that scurries and swarms in the water, and every sort of bird—each producing offspring of the same kind. And God saw that it was good. Then God blessed them, saying, "Be fruitful and multiply. Let the fish fill the seas, and let the birds multiply on the earth." And evening passed and morning came, marking the fifth day.

GENESIS 1:20–23

By the end of the fourth creation day, God had already made everything He knew would be needed for all the different kinds of animals to live on Earth. He made the earth itself and had separated dry land from the water, and He had stocked the earth with plenty of water for the animals to live in and to drink. He had provided the sunlight that is so vital to the growth of plants that would feed the animals and that would supply them with oxygen to breathe.

God had prepared everything perfectly for the animals He was about to create on the fifth and sixth days of creation. It was now time for Him to create what we now call the *animal kingdom*. He started His work of populating the world with animals by creating fish and birds.

Natural Kingdoms

The Bible doesn't list every type of living thing God created. It doesn't even list what humans would later call kingdoms. Maybe that's because He just wanted us to know the basics of creation. Whatever the reason, we can know that He created everything that lives on Earth today.

Not everything that lives on Earth is considered an animal. Over the years, scientists have broken down the world of all living things into what they call *kingdoms*. All living things are divided into five kingdoms: the *Monera kingdom* (includes single-celled creatures called *bacteria*), the *Protista kingdom* (some kinds of algae and single-celled creatures called *protozoa*), the *Fungi kingdom* (molds, spores, and mushrooms), the *plant kingdom*, and the *animal kingdom*.

On the fifth day of creation, God began making the animal kingdom. The animal kingdom includes worms, insects, arachnids (animals with eight legs, like spiders and scorpions), mollusks (such as clams, oysters, and octopuses), crustaceans, fish, reptiles, amphibians, birds, and mammals. It also includes creatures you might not have known are animals—creatures such as sponges and corals.

All these living creatures have some special traits in common that make them animals. All of them are made up of many individual cells, and all of them rely in some way or another on other living things for their nourishment. Also, most animals eat their food and digest it inside themselves.

Moving Down the Family Tree

Scientists not only break down all living things into the five kingdoms, but they also break down the animal kingdom into smaller groups called *phyla* (the plural of *phylum*). Most scientists believe there are 38 animal phyla and that most animal species belong to the nine biggest of them.

Each phylum includes smaller groups of animals called *classes*. Classes of animals are then divided into smaller groups called *orders*. Orders are divided into *families* (and sometimes subfamilies), and each family includes a number of different *genera* (the plural of *genus*). Finally, each genus is broken down into one or more *species* of animal.

A red-billed tropic bird photographed over the Caribbean Sea.

Fish and birds—the animals God made on the fifth day of creation—are part of the phylum *Chordata*, which includes all animals that are considered vertebrates. *Vertebrates* are animals that have backbones. *Invertebrates*, on the other hand, are animals that don't have backbones—like crabs, spiders, and insects. Those three animals are called *arthropods,* and they belong to the phylum *Arthropoda*.

Birds all belong to one class of animals called *Aves*. But there are several classes of fish living in the world today.

A blue-spotted stingray photographed off Thailand.

Fish's Big Place in the Animal Kingdom

Altogether there are about 28,000 different species of fish populating the world's waters—with new species still being discovered every year. Some *ichthyologists* (scientists who study fish) say there may be many thousands more fish species yet to be discovered and named.

If you were to look at a chart of different kinds of fish, you would see at the top of their family tree the *superclasses* and *classes*, then what are called *subclasses*. The subclasses are followed by *infraclasses*. If you kept moving down the chart, you'd see the *superorders* of fish, followed by the *orders*, then the *superfamilies* and then the *families*.

There are three superclasses of fish living today, and each of them includes several classes. The biggest superclass of fish is *Osteichthyes* (fish with skeletons made of bone). This class of fish includes the subclass *Achtinopterygii*, which scientists call "ray-finned" fish. If you can't pronounce the word *Achtinopterygii*, don't worry. You can just think of them as typical fish, because for the most part they look like you'd expect a fish to look. This class of fish includes around 27,000 species, making it not only the largest class of fish but the largest class of vertebrates.

The *Agnatha* superclass of fish is known for having skeletons made of cartilage rather than bone, like most fish. They also don't have jaws. This class includes lampreys and hagfish. And here's something really strange about this class of fish: they have digestive systems, just like any other fish, but they don't have stomachs!

The *Chondrichthyes* superclass of fish, which also has skeletons made of cartilage, includes sharks and rays. This class of fish includes some species you have no doubt heard about, including the whale shark, the largest fish alive on Earth today, and the great white shark.

There are literally hundreds of families of fish, but one-third of all species belong to the nine largest families. The family with the most species (at about 2,400) is called the *Cyprinidae* family, which includes carps and minnows. Since goldfish are carps, they belong to this family of fish.

To help you better understand the basics of how scientists classify fish, take a look at the chart below, which shows you where a common goldfish fits in the animal kingdom:

- Kingdom: *Animalia* (all animals)
- Phylum: *Chordata* (animals with backbones)
- Class: *Achtinopterygii* (all ray-finned fish)
- Order: *Cypriniformes* (carps, minnows, roaches, and their relatives)
- Family: *Cyprinidae* (carps, minnows, and barbs)
- Genus: *Carassius* (crucian carps)
- Species: *Carassius auratus* (goldfish)

RECORD BREAKING

At up to 40 feet long and weighing up to 15 tons, the whale shark is the world's biggest fish. If you ever saw a whale shark, you wouldn't need to worry about being attacked, even if you were in the water with it. A whale shark eats only *plankton*—tiny plants and animals that live in the sea—and other small organisms, which it catches by taking water into its huge mouth and then straining out the food through its gills. In fact, it has been reported that whale sharks are gentle creatures that sometimes seem to enjoy playing with divers.

A diver swims with a whale shark in the Indian Ocean.

What Makes a Fish a Fish?

Fish are some of the most amazing members of the animal kingdom. All fish are vertebrates, which means they have backbones. All birds and mammals, including human beings, are also vertebrates, but more than half of all known species of vertebrates living in the world today are fish.

On the fifth day of creation, God made fish and many other forms of life that live in the water. That included many types of life that are not fish, even though they may have some of the same characteristics as fish. Different species of jellyfish, starfish, shellfish, sea anemones, coral, crustaceans (crabs, shrimps, lobsters, and others), and thousands of other animals also live in the earth's water, but they aren't fish.

So what makes a fish a fish? Fish come in every size, color, and shape you can imagine—and some you probably can't—but they all have certain things in common. . .other than having a backbone, that is. All fish are *cold-blooded*, meaning that their body temperature adjusts to the temperature of the water they live in. All fish have gills that absorb oxygen from the water into their bloodstreams. All fish have fins, though some species have more than others. And most fish have scales that protect their bodies.

THAT'S AMAZING!

Even though there's a lot of mystery around what kinds of fish and other sea creatures live in the deepest part of the world's oceans, scientists know that the record for fish living in the deepest waters goes to a type of fish in the brotulid family. These fish live in the ocean at depths of 23,000 feet or more. One species of fish—with the tongue-twisting scientific name of *Abyssobrotula galatheae*—was captured in the Puerto Rican Trench from an amazing depth of almost 27,500 feet—or more than five miles down. Most fish living at these depths have lost the use of their eyes—if they have eyes at all—simply because sunlight can't penetrate that deep into the ocean.

Where Fish Live

Fish live in just about any area of the world where you can find bodies of water. Some live in the salt water of the world's oceans and seas. But many also live in freshwater lakes, rivers, streams, and other bodies of water. Some freshwater fish live in slow-moving or still water (in lakes and ponds), but others tend to live in fast-moving streams and rivers. Still other species of fish live in what is called *brackish* water, which is a mixture of salt water and fresh water found in some coastal areas. One place you'll never find a fish living is in very salty bodies of water, like the Great Salt Lake in Utah.

Some types of fish live in places where the conditions would kill most other forms of life. There are fish that live in streams and pools in caves where no sunlight reaches them. Some fish live in the deepest parts of the ocean, several miles down. Some fish live in desert ponds and streams that dry up every year. These fish have the amazing ability to bury themselves in the mud, hibernate for up to two years, then swim free when the water returns. Some fish even live under the polar ice caps!

Can you imagine walking down the street and seeing a fish crawling along in front of you? That's exactly what happens sometimes in some neighborhoods in Florida, where a really strange fish called the *walking catfish* is sometimes seen crawling on dry land from one body of water to another. This weird species of fish has the ability to "walk" (actually, they crawl using their pectoral fins as legs) on dry land for a short time and breathe air as it moves from one body of water to another. Walking catfish first came to the United States in the 1960s, when they were imported from Asia for home aquariums.

How Fish Breathe

A fish's gills are amazingly designed organs. The gills are made up of tiny threadlike strands filled with tiny blood vessels. The fish breathes by taking water in through its open mouth and then forcing the water over the filaments when it closes its mouth. The filaments absorb the oxygen and move it into the fish's bloodstream.

Even though all fish have gills to collect oxygen from the water, some fish also take oxygen out of the air, using specially designed organs that do the same work your lungs do. Some species of lungfish can bury themselves in the mud when the body of water they live in dries up. These fish can survive on oxygen from the air for up to two years or until the water returns.

Some kinds of fish have labyrinth organs that they use to breathe air from the atmosphere so that they can survive in oxygen-poor water. They still have gills just like any other fish, and they get most of their oxygen from the water. These fish are called *labyrinth fish*, and they include the betta (or Siamese fighting fish), a fish you can find in just about any pet store or aquarium shop.

How Fish Reproduce "After Their Own Kind"

When God created the different species of fish, He designed them to reproduce in a variety of ways. Most fish reproduce by laying or scattering their eggs in the water. This process is called *spawning*, and it happens when the female fish releases her eggs into the water and the male fertilizes them with his sperm. Some fish give birth to live babies. That means that the male fish must deposit his sperm inside the female fish, where her eggs are fertilized and later grow into baby fish that are born alive. Most fish leave their eggs or young to fend for themselves, but some are very good parents that protect their nests and babies until their offspring are able to take care of themselves.

Most fish reproduce in the same water they live in their whole lives. But some fish begin their lives in fresh water, migrate to salt water, where they spend most of their lives, then return to fresh water to spawn. These are called *anadromous* fish, and they include salmon, smelt, shad, striped bass, sturgeon, and others. On the other hand, there are fish that are born in salt water but live most of their lives in fresh water, only to return to salt water to spawn. These are called *catadromous* fish, and they include most kinds of eels.

DID YOU KNOW...?

While most fish lay their eggs or give live birth to their young and then pay no attention to them (other than to eat them, in some cases!), some species of fish are very good parents. For example, many species from the cichlid (pronounced "sick-lid") family—some of which are kept in freshwater aquariums as pets—are some of the most devoted, protective parents in all creation. Some species of cichlids fiercely guard their eggs and young from any and all predators—even those that are far bigger than they are! Probably the best examples are the mouthbreeders, which care for their eggs and young by carrying them in their mouths.

EXPLORING THE WORLD OF FISH

If you're interested in exploring the world of fish, you don't need to go any farther than your local pet store or aquarium shop. When you go, take a pencil and notepad, and as

you look at the different kinds of fish, write down what you see, including the name of the species. Then go to your library—or log on to the internet—and see what you can learn about the fish you've just seen: what they eat, how they reproduce, where they live in the wild. As you do these things, you'll learn to understand and appreciate God's creativity in making these fish you've just seen.

Birds, Birds Everywhere!

Birds live all over the world. They are found on every continent and in almost every kind of climate. Leading the world with the most species of birds—3,200—is South America. That includes the nations of Colombia, Bolivia, and Peru, each of which is home to around 1,700 species. About 2,900 species of birds live in Asia, and Africa is home to about 2,300. North America—which includes the United States and Canada—accounts for about 2,000 species, with another 1,000 living in Europe. There are even 65 kinds of birds living in Antarctica!

Of course, there are far more kinds of birds living in more ordinary climates where there are no extremely hot or extremely cold temperatures. But God also has designed and equipped certain birds to live in places where it's hard to imagine any living thing surviving for very long.

Birds are found in the hottest, driest deserts. Others are found in the coldest parts of the Arctic and Antarctic. Different kinds of birds live in open grasslands, in forests and jungles, on cliff faces and mountaintops, and on riverbanks and seashores. Some birds like to make their homes in man-made structures like barns, mine shafts, and the roofs of houses.

Some birds live only near or in water. These kinds of birds, which are called *aquatic birds*, also get most or all of their food from the water. Some species of aquatic birds, such as loons, tend to live near freshwater lakes, and some tend to live near salt water. Some aquatic birds live near both salt water and fresh water. Birds like ducks, geese, and swans—birds called *waterfowl*—live near freshwater lakes, ponds, and marshes.

Birds that live in different kinds of environments look and behave very differently from one another. The easiest differences for you to see are the bird's size, body shape, color, beak or bill shape, and the length of the legs and neck. None of these differences happened by accident. They happened because the same God who created the environment where the bird lives also designed each bird to live in the environment He placed it in.

Doesn't he look cold? This chinstrap penguin of Antarctica is named for the black line that runs under his beak.

Tiny hummingbirds have long, thin beaks they use to suck nectar from delicate flowers.

Large macaws have short, tough beaks they use to crack nuts.

Sparrows are common birds, and a good example of passerines, birds that perch.

The common loon is a duck-like bird of North America.

Some turkeys are raised on farms. This is a wild turkey, showing off his plumage (tail feathers).

The budgie, a type of parakeet, is a common pet bird.

The Bird Family Tree

Earlier you read about the long and complicated "family tree" of the world's fish. Birds have their own family tree too, but it isn't nearly as large or complicated as that of fish.

Like all fish, all birds are part of the phylum *Chordata*, which means they are all animals with backbones. But unlike fish, all birds belong to just one class of animals. That class is called *Aves*. *Ornithologists*—scientists who study birds—have placed birds into about two dozen groups called *orders*. Those orders are divided into about 160 families, which are then grouped into birds of the same genus. Finally, the genus is divided into the different species of birds.

There are about 10,000 known species of birds living all over the world today, and more than half of them are from the order *Passeriformes*. They are more often called *passerines*, and they are from the order scientists have listed as *perching birds*. These birds' toes and legs are designed so that they can balance themselves on tree limbs, twigs, and telephone wires. Common birds like sparrows, finches, warblers, crows, blackbirds, thrushes, and swallows are all considered perching birds.

Other orders of birds include kinds of birds you have probably either seen or heard of. The order *Anseriformes*, which includes ducks, geese, swans, and other kinds of waterfowl. The bald eagle, as well as other kinds of birds of prey like hawks and falcons, belongs to the order *Falconiformes*. Turkeys and chickens, both important birds for food, are from the order *Galliformes*. And the parrots, macaws, parakeets, and several other kinds of birds you see at your local pet store? They are from the order *Psittaciformes*.

When you get down the family tree for birds to the branch scientists call the *genus*, then you'll start to see how much certain kinds of birds are very much like other kinds in that genus. For example, the white stork and the black stork are from the same genus (called *Ciconia*) and look very much alike (except for the color), but they are two different kinds of birds.

To help you better understand how scientists have put

together the family tree for birds, take a look at the following chart. It will show you where the American robin, a bird you have probably seen many times, fits in:

- Kingdom: *Animalia* (all animals)
- Phylum: *Chordata* (animals with backbones)
- Class: *Aves* (all birds)
- Order: *Passeriformes* (perching birds)
- Family: *Turdidae* (all thrushes)
- Genus: *Turdus* (similar thrushes)
- Species: *Turdus migratorius* (the American robin)

The American robin

What Makes a Bird a Bird?

God created birds in many different sizes, shapes, and colors. The tiny bee hummingbird is the smallest bird known. It measures less than 2.5 inches long when fully grown and weighs less than .10 ounces. Ostriches, on the other hand, are the world's largest bird. Ostriches can grow to eight feet tall and can weigh more than 300 pounds.

But no matter how big or small a certain kind of bird is, no matter what color its feathers are, and no matter where it lives or how it eats or nests, it has certain things in common with all other birds.

Like fish, birds are vertebrates, and that means they have backbones. But instead of fins and scales, birds have wings, feathers, and a beak (or bill) with no teeth. Birds are also *warm-blooded*, which means that their body temperature stays pretty much the same all the time. All birds reproduce by laying eggs.

The bee hummingbird—the smallest known bird—lives in Cuba. This is a female, which is slightly larger than the male.

Most species of birds can fly, and they use that ability to hunt for food, to escape predators (including other birds sometimes), and to migrate from one place to another so they can get away from weather that is too cold or too hot. Birds that can fly are designed to be some of the world's greatest athletes. They have strong, hollow bones, powerful muscles, and strong hearts and lungs. They also have amazingly designed wings and powerful flight muscles that give them the ability to take off, to stay in the air, and to reach sometimes amazing speeds in midair.

But do you know what one characteristic sets birds apart from all other animals? It's not the fact that they all reproduce by laying eggs. Most species of fish, reptiles, and amphibians—as well as a few mammals—lay eggs. So do insects and many other living creatures. It's not the fact that they all have wings and that most of them can fly. Bats are mammals, but they have wings and can fly. So can most insects. It's not even the fact that they all have beaks or bills.

RECORD BREAKING

A peregrine falcon snatches a smaller bird in flight.

The peregrine falcon, which lives almost everywhere on Earth, is not only the world's fastest-flying bird but also the fastest creature of any kind on Earth today. Peregrines can fly at speeds of well over 200 miles per hour. They use their speed to hunt for food. They swoop from great heights to catch prey on the ground and other birds in midair. Peregrines eat mostly medium-sized birds, but they also sometimes eat small mammals and reptiles and insects.

If you want to know for certain if an animal is a bird, remember this: *If it has feathers, it's a bird!* In all the animal kingdom, only birds have feathers. Not only that, *all* birds have feathers!

God didn't put feathers on birds just to make them look pretty. Different types of feathers on a bird's body serve different purposes. The long, wide feathers on the bird's wings and tail allow the bird to fly (the tail feathers help the bird to steer itself while in flight), and the softer feathers that grow close to the skin help insulate the bird from heat or cold. Some male birds have big, colorful feathers they use to attract their mates, while the females usually have duller-colored feathers that help them to blend into their surroundings while they nest. That way they can escape the notice of predators that like to eat eggs—or the mother bird herself.

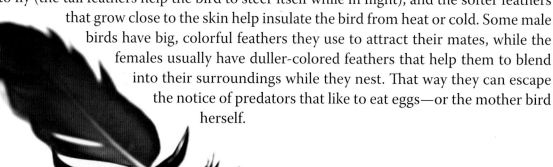

You probably know that ostriches can't fly. Their bodies are too heavy and their wings are too small for them to even attempt flying. But did you know there are actually 40 species of birds living on Earth today that can't fly? The list also includes several different species of kiwis, which live in New Zealand, as well as the emu, which is a native of Australia. Penguins, which live in the earth's Southern Hemisphere, are also flightless birds, but they use their wings for swimming. In case you're wondering, chickens don't fit on the list of flightless birds because they can actually fly.

Drivers in New Zealand see this sign, to warn them of kiwis ahead!

The southern masked-weaver is an African bird that weaves its nest from grass, reeds, and other natural materials.

How Birds Reproduce

All birds reproduce by laying eggs with hard shells. The number of eggs the female bird lays at one time depends on the species. Some birds lay one egg per nesting, while others lay more than a dozen at a time. All birds' eggs are fertilized during mating while they are still inside the female bird's body.

Most birds build nests to protect their eggs from weather and predators. What the nest looks like and where the bird builds it depends on the species of bird. Many birds nest in trees, but others nest on the ground or underground. Some birds like to nest in man-made structures like housetops, gutters, barns and sheds, and other places. Some birds weave beautiful nests of grass, twigs, feathers, and other materials, but some nest in hollowed-out trees. Other kinds of birds, like eagles, nest in high treetops, while others just dig out a hole in the sand or dirt to nest. Some birds even nest in underground burrows.

Almost all birds sit on their eggs to keep them warm until they hatch. Most bird "couples" stay together during the nesting time and take turns sitting on the eggs so both the male and the female have a chance to feed. That is not true for all birds, though. Male emus do all the sitting and also care for the babies once they hatch. The male emperor penguin cares for his mate's egg during its incubation period. Once the egg has hatched and the female penguin returns from the sea where she has been feeding, she begins helping care for the newly hatched chick.

When most baby birds first hatch, they are completely dependent on their parents for food. Both parents feed the young, whose mouths are always open, waiting for Mom and Dad to feed them. Some birds feed their young by eating and partly digesting the food, then vomiting it into their chicks' mouths. That's called *regurgitation*, and although it might sound kinda gross, for the baby birds it's as tasty and nutritious as a big pancake breakfast is to you!

Some baby birds are able to eat on their own almost as soon as they hatch. Baby ducks, geese, chickens, quails, and other types of birds get up and walk soon after they hatch, but they stay close to their mothers, who protect them and take them to places where they can find food.

THAT'S WEIRD!

The killdeer is an amazing—and really noisy—bird that uses a really strange method for protecting its nest. When a predator, looking for a quick egg breakfast, gets too close to the killdeer's nest, the mother will use a broken-wing act to distract the predator. The bird will walk away from the nest, then start flopping around on the ground and squawking as if it is injured and can't fly. Once the mother has distracted the predator into thinking it has found an easy meal, she suddenly seems to get better. She then flies away and circles the area before she returns to her nest.

THAT'S AMAZING!

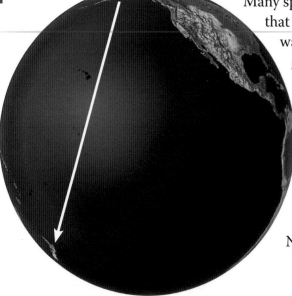

Many species of birds are *migratory*, which means that they travel during certain seasons to find warmer weather or to mate. In 2007 a bar-tailed godwit—a wading bird that mates in the Arctic coasts and tundra—made an amazing journey in an amazingly short period of time. Scientists tracked the bird as if flew south from Alaska to New Zealand—a distance of 7,145 miles—in just nine days. This amazing bird never stopped to eat, drink, or rest, and it lost more than half its body weight by the time it touched down in New Zealand.

Eating Like a Bird

Ever hear the phrase "eats like a bird"? That is usually what people say about someone who doesn't eat very much. But the truth about birds is that most of them consume a lot of food for their size. They have to eat a lot because they use up so much energy flying.

What a bird eats depends on the kind of bird it is. Many birds eat almost nothing but fruit and seeds, while others eat green plants. Birds such as hummingbirds eat nectar they find in flowers. Many species of birds eat insects and other bugs. Some birds of prey eat fish, small reptiles, and rodents, while others eat mammals and other birds they catch. Some birds, like vultures, are scavengers that eat only the bodies of dead animals.

The size and shape of a bird can tell you a lot about how it finds food and how it eats it. Every bird is equipped with everything it needs to gather or catch the kind of food it eats. For example, if a bird has long legs and a long neck—like a crane or flamingo—it probably spends most of its time walking on land or wading in water. Birds with long legs need long necks so they can reach food on the ground or in the water.

Hummingbirds have long, thin beaks and slender tongues they use to dip into flowers to gather nectar. Swallows, swifts, and other birds that eat insects have short beaks and wide mouths that are perfect for catching flying insects. Parrots and other seed-eating birds have powerful, curved beaks that help them in cracking open nuts to eat.

Eww, gross! The deader the better for scavenging birds like vultures.

These ducks aren't shy—they're looking for food underwater!

Birds of prey, such as eagles, hawks, ospreys, and owls, use their sharp eyesight and hearing to find food. They also use their strong claws (or *talons*) and hooked beaks to kill and eat their prey once they catch it. Some species of owls swallow their prey whole once they catch it, then vomit up the bones, fur, and other parts of the animal they can't digest.

Pelicans, geese, and swans all swim well and also have short legs and long necks that allow them to submerge their heads in the water to find food. Other water birds—such as cormorants—are considered diving birds. Their bodies are shaped a lot like torpedoes, and that allows them to dive deep and fast into the water to catch fish.

EXPLORING THE WORLD OF BIRDS

Whether you live in a big city or out in the country, you live in a place where you can see many types of birds. One good way to get a good look at the species of birds in your area is to set out a bird feeder. . .then just watch who comes to have a free meal! When birds come to eat at your feeder, take a good look at them—and take pictures of them if you can—then see if you can identify which species of birds live near you.

Why Fish and Birds Are Important to You

The Bible tells us that the very first animals God created were fish (and other creatures that live

Many of the eggs we eat come from large farms. These eggs are being processed on a conveyor belt.

in the water) and birds. When you look at the variety of fish living in the earth's bodies of water and at the different kinds of birds that live on Earth, you can see that God really likes variety.

But there's something else we can learn about God as we look at the living things He placed on Earth. As you will read later on in this book, God didn't just create all the animals that live on Earth so that He could have a huge zoo and aquarium to enjoy for Himself. God created all these things for the benefit of the most valuable and important part of His creation—us!

The fish and birds God created are important gifts to us humans for a lot of reasons. First of all, fish and birds are an important source of food for people in nearly all cultures. Fish are plentiful in many parts of the world and serve as a source of protein as well as useful fatty acids that help keep people's hearts healthy and operating properly.

Some kinds of birds are important sources of food. Can you remember the last time you had a chicken dinner with your family? Or when you had scrambled eggs or an omelet for breakfast? And you know that every Thanksgiving holiday many Americans cook a big turkey dinner to celebrate with their friends and families. People also often eat geese, pheasants, ducks, grouse, quail, and other game birds. In some parts of the world, people even eat the meat of emus and ostriches.

People also enjoy fish and birds for recreation and as pets. Both saltwater and freshwater sport fishing are popular in many parts of the world. So is hunting for birds. Many people in different parts of the world enjoy keeping aquariums in their homes so that they can enjoy caring for and breeding different types of fish.

Colorful birds like parrots, cockatiels, parakeets, and other species are kept as pets because they are pretty to look at. Some birds are also popular because they can be taught to copy human speech.

Birds are intelligent pets that enjoy bright, noisy toys.

Some people also enjoy just going out and watching birds in the wild. These people call their activity *birding*—even though you probably know it better as *bird-watching*. Some bird-watchers just go out with a pair of binoculars to enjoy seeing birds in their natural habitat, but some enjoy taking cameras along so they can collect pictures of wild birds.

So the next time you enjoy a nice fish or chicken or turkey dinner, or the next time you have eggs with your breakfast, don't forget to thank God for both His creativity and for providing you with the foods you eat. And the next time you go out fishing with your family or watch fish in an aquarium (at home or anywhere else) or watch birds enjoying life in the wild, remember that it was God who made these creatures for you to enjoy.

A bird book, binoculars, and a camera are nice for bird-watching—but not necessary. You can observe birds anywhere at any time!

CHAPTER 7

DAY 6, PART I
ALL THE LAND ANIMALS

Then God said, "Let the earth produce every sort of animal, each producing offspring of the same kind—livestock, small animals that scurry along the ground, and wild animals." And that is what happened. God made all sorts of wild animals, livestock, and small animals, each able to produce offspring of the same kind. And God saw that it was good.

GENESIS 1:24–25

When the sixth day of creation started, the earth had already been completely formed and filled with all kinds of plants, fish, and birds. God's next step in preparing our planet for us humans to live on was to create the different kinds of animals that live on land.

When you think of the animals that live on land, your mind probably goes to the animals that people are closest to—like dogs, cats, and horses. Some animals just seem to be designed for people to enjoy in special ways. Many people keep dogs and cats in their homes and treat them like members of the family. Other people like horses because they can train them and ride them and enjoy spending time with them.

But many of the land animals God created are important to humans for other reasons. Many land animals are sources of food. Other animals help people do their work. Amazingly enough, God had a purpose for *all* the land animals He created—from the biggest mammals (like elephants) to the tiniest insects (like ants).

Land Mammals. . .Including You!

Did you know that you are a mammal? It's true! People are mammals because they share some of the same features as animals like horses, cats, dogs, cattle, and all the rest of the 4,000 to 5,000 kinds of mammals living in the world today.

Land mammals come in a large variety of sizes, shapes, and colors. The smallest mammals are so tiny that it's likely you wouldn't see them if you were standing right next to them. The largest land mammals—the elephants—would be hard for anyone to miss! (The blue whale is actually the world's largest mammal, but it lives in the ocean and was probably created on the fifth day of creation.)

Some of the land mammals God created are known for their physical beauty. Who can't look at a Bengal tiger or a

This picture is about the same size as a real mouse.

leopard and appreciate how beautiful and majestic God made those big cats? But some animals will never win any beauty contest. In fact, some land mammals are among the funniest-looking creatures in the entire animal kingdom. One example is the star-nosed mole, a species commonly found living near swamps and ponds in the eastern part of the United States. The star-nosed mole has a snout made up of 22 fleshy tentacles that make its nose look like a starfish with too many arms.

One of the weirdest-looking—and most misunderstood—land mammals is a small primate (the same family of animals as apes and monkeys) called the aye-aye. The aye-aye, which uses its long, slender middle finger to find and scoop insects to eat out of trees, is far from the most handsome animal in the world (go ahead and look it up!). It has large, yellowish eyes and long, slender fingers. The residents of Madagascar, where it lives, often kill it because they

The aye-aye is related to monkeys but looks kind of like a cat—until you see those long, skinny fingers.

think it is an evil spirit or a sign of bad luck. That is one reason the aye-aye is an endangered species.

Not only does the star-nosed mole have a strange face, but look at the size of those paws! They're extra big to help him dig through the soil.

RECORD BREAKING

You probably already know that the elephant is the biggest land animal on Earth today. But there are actually several species of elephants, including the biggest one of all: the African bush elephant. This species of elephant can weigh 225 pounds when it is born, and most of them grow to around 20 to 24 feet long and 10 to 12 feet tall at the shoulder, and weigh between 13,000 and 20,000 pounds. The biggest African bush elephant on record weighed 27,060 pounds and stood almost 14 feet tall.

DID YOU KNOW. . . ?

You have probably heard that no two people have exactly the same fingerprints. (Yes, that means your fingerprints are yours and yours alone.) But did you know that each giraffe and each zebra also has its own one-of-a-kind identifiers? It's true! No two giraffes have the exact same pattern of spots, and no two zebras have the same pattern of stripes. That means that each giraffe and each zebra is a one-of-a-kind creation with its own identity—just like you!

Where Land Mammals Live

Land mammals live in almost all kinds of environments. Polar bears and some kinds of seals live in the coldest parts of the world, while camels and other animals live in some of the hottest. Moles and other burrowing animals live underground, and bats live in caves and other places where they can keep out of the sunlight during the day. Other animals live in forests and jungles, in deserts and open fields, and in mountains and valleys.

Like the other kinds of life God created, the way different mammals look and behave can tell you a lot about the kind of surroundings they live in. God equipped the cold-weather specialists like polar bears with thick fur and layers of fat to help keep them warm. He also equipped animals that live in hotter areas with thick fur and skin that help insulate them from the heat. And He gave the animals that live in warmer areas of the world the ability to pant or sweat to release extra heat from their bodies.

God also designed different animals to eat different kinds of food. He gave animals that eat only plants the kind of teeth and digestive systems that work best for eating grass, grains, fruits, and vegetables. These mammals are called *herbivores*. He also gave animals that eat meat—they are called *carnivores*—strong jaws and sharp teeth that work best for eating the meat from other animals. God also equipped some carnivores with the speed and strength they need to hunt their prey.

A female cheetah chases a young gazelle in Kenya.

Without a doubt, the cheetah is the top track star out of all the land mammals. Cheetahs, which are found in Saharan Africa, can go from 0 to 45 miles an hour in less than two seconds and can reach top speeds of up to 70 miles per hour. Cheetahs are built for speed. They have long, slender legs and a tail they use for balance when they make quick cuts. They use their amazing speed and agility to catch their prey, which includes impalas, gazelles, rabbits, birds, and other small animals. Even though cheetahs are fast, they can only reach their top speeds in short bursts.

The Land Mammal Family Tree

Scientists have classified and named mammals the same way they have classified and named the fish and birds that live on Earth. The different kinds of mammals are broken down into one class—called *Mammalia*—that includes about 20 different orders of animals—give or take an order or two, depending on who you talk to. Each order of mammals is broken down into families and sometimes subfamilies, and each of the families is broken down into one or more genera (remember, that's the plural of *genus*). Each genus includes a certain number of kinds of animals that are all very much alike in many ways.

The Indiana bat is a tiny mammal!

This will probably surprise you, but nearly one-fourth of all species of mammals have the ability to fly. Strange but true! There are about 985 species of bats, which accounts for just over 23 percent of all known kinds of mammals. Though there are a few mammals that can glide through the air—such as flying squirrels and flying possums—bats are the only mammals that can really fly. Most bats are *insectivores*, meaning they eat bugs, but some eat nectar and pollen, while others eat fish, frogs, lizards, small rodents, birds, or other bats. A few species of bats drink fresh blood.

A chimp gets a piggyback ride from her human handler, who is preparing the animal to return to the wild.

Scientists have placed us humans in the same order of mammals as apes and monkeys. This order of mammals is called *Primates*. That means that out of the entire animal kingdom, the mammals that are most like us are the apes—including gorillas, chimpanzees, and orangutans—and monkeys, as well as other members of that order. While these kinds of animals lack some of the special traits God gave only humans (you'll read more about that in chapter 8), they are like us in many ways. For one thing, they are among the most intelligent animals in all creation.

It might surprise you to know that the order of mammals with the most species is *Rodentia* or rodents. There are as many as 2,277 different kinds of rodents living in the world today. Mice

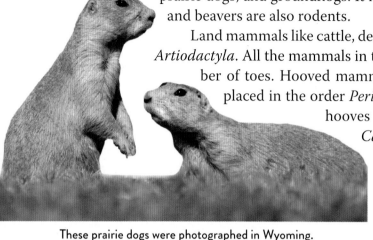

and rats are rodents, and so are squirrels, chipmunks, gophers, hamsters, gerbils, guinea pigs, prairie dogs, and groundhogs. It may surprise you to know that porcupines and beavers are also rodents.

Land mammals like cattle, deer, pigs, and camels are placed in the order *Artiodactyla*. All the mammals in this order have hooves with an even number of toes. Hooved mammals like horses, donkeys, and zebras are placed in the order *Perissodactyla*. All animals in this order have hooves with an odd number of toes. The order *Carnivora* includes meat-eating mammals like cats (the ones that live in the wild, like lions, tigers, and cougars, as well as cats people keep as pets), dogs (including wolves, foxes, and coyotes), bears, raccoons, and many others.

Some kinds of animals are placed in

These prairie dogs were photographed in Wyoming. They generally live west of the Mississippi River.

Did you know that male donkeys are called jacks, and female donkeys jennies?

smaller orders because they have some very unusual traits. For example, the order *Marsupialia* includes only animals that carry their babies in a pouch—like the kangaroo. And the order *Proboscidea* is made up of only one family of mammals: elephants! It might make you laugh to read this, but the name *Proboscidea* means "eats with the nose." That name comes from the fact that elephants use their noses—which are really called *trunks*—to gather food and put it in their mouths.

The opossum is a marsupial because—like the kangaroo—it carries its babies in a pouch. But these babies are big enough to ride on Mom's back!

What Makes a Mammal a Mammal?

Like fish and birds, mammals are all part of the phylum *Chordata*. Remember, most animals from that phylum are considered vertebrates, which means they have backbones. All mammals are also warm-blooded. Remember, *warm-blooded* means that an animal's body is designed to stay at a certain temperature, no matter how warm or cold it is where it lives.

But there are a lot of animals living today that have spinal columns and are warm-blooded. Fish and birds—the first animals God created—all have backbones. So do all reptiles and amphibians. And birds are warm-blooded, just like mammals. So to know what makes a mammal a mammal, we're going to have to narrow things down a bit.

So, what else do you think all mammals have in common?

First of all, every mammal has hair or fur. It's pretty easy to see hair on most mammals. Most dogs and cats have thick hair and fur all over their bodies. So do bears, cattle, horses, and many other mammals. Even mammals whose hair is hard to see have hair. That includes mammals that live in water, like dolphins and whales. Even though you can't easily see hair on these animals, it's there—it's just really small.

Not only do all mammals have hair or fur, but they are the only animals on Earth that do. "Wait a minute!" you might be saying. "I've seen pictures of tarantulas, and they are covered in hair!"

RECORD BREAKING

The smallest mammal in the world is the Kitti's hog-nosed bat, which lives in Thailand and feeds on small insects. This tiny bat grows to only 1.14 to 1.3 inches long and weighs just .07 ounces when it is fully grown. At that size, it is a lot smaller than a lot of insects. The Kitti's hog-nosed bat barely beats out Savi's pygmy shrew—also known as the white-toothed pygmy shrew—as the world's smallest mammal. These tiny creatures, which are found in southern Europe, grow to less than 1.75 inches long and weigh less than .10 ounces as adults.

Hair on a dolphin? You'll have to look very closely. . .

Breakfast time for a kid—of the goat variety.

It's true that tarantulas and other creatures that aren't mammals *look* like they are covered in hair. But what seems like hair on a tarantula isn't really hair at all. Real hair is made up of dead strands of a substance called *keratin*. It's the same stuff your hair and fingernails and the hooves and horns of animals are made of. What looks like hair on a tarantula actually contains living parts of the spider.

Another way that all mammals are alike is that they feed their babies with milk that comes from the mother's body. From the biggest elephant in the world to the tiniest mouse or bat, every mammal mother gives her baby the nourishment it needs to grow in the form of milk. Because mammal babies rely on their mother's milk to live and grow, mammal mothers all care for their young.

So there you have it! If an animal is a warm-blooded creature with a backbone and has hair on its body and feeds its young with milk, then it's a mammal! If an animal lacks any of those things, then it's something else.

THAT'S WEIRD!

The platypus is not only strange looking; it can also be dangerous. Male platypuses can sting other creatures with a venom that comes through a sharp spur on their ankles.

Ever seen a duck-billed platypus? Other than having a strange name and also looking really funny, the platypus, which lives in eastern Australia, is one of only a few mammals that lays eggs instead of giving birth to its young. When scientists from Europe first saw the platypus—which has a mouth like a duck, a tail like a beaver, and feet like an otter—they thought someone was playing a joke on them. But it was real! And it's one of the weirdest-looking mammals God created!

Mammal Moms

Nearly all mammal mothers carry their babies inside them before giving birth. The amount of time the baby spends in its mother's body before it is born is called the *gestation period*. The amount of time it takes for the mammal baby to develop before it is born depends on the kind of mammal. Baby opossums are inside their mother's body just 12 days before they are born. And baby hamsters take 16 days to develop. Human babies are born about 266 days after the mother's egg is fertilized. The longest gestation period in the mammal world? The Indian elephant, at an amazing 624 days!

As a group, mammal mothers are just about the best in all creation. They care for their young, protect them from predators and other dangers, and, of course, they feed them every day. Because all baby mammals rely on their mother's milk to live and grow, the mother must care for the young at least until they are able to feed themselves and survive on their own. That means that mammal moms spend all of their time caring for their babies. The length of time a mammal mother cares for its young depends on the kind of animal. Some mammals—like certain kinds of rodents—care for their young for just a few weeks.

Nearly all mammal babies, including humans, have baby teeth or *milk teeth*. That makes it easier for the mother to feed its young the milk they need to live and grow. The exception to this rule in the mammal world is anteaters and a few other species of mammals that never grow teeth.

Reptiles: Land Animals with Scales

Out of all the animals that live on Earth, reptiles probably have the hardest time being accepted by humans. Some people are afraid of reptiles. Maybe it has something to do with the fact that all reptiles are covered with scales. Or maybe people just don't like animals that crawl or slither on the ground.

Even though some kinds of reptiles are poisonous—like some snakes and lizards such Gila monsters—they are still important members the animal kingdom. Reptiles are helpful humans in several ways. Many reptiles eat rodents and other "pests," which helps farmers and other people who grow food for humans. In some cultures people eat certain reptiles, and some people enjoy keeping them as pets.

There are about 8,200 to 9,000 different species of reptiles living on Earth today. That includes many species each of turtles, snakes, crocodiles, lizards, and others. Reptiles live on every continent on Earth except Antarctica. Reptiles come as small as the dwarf gecko, which grows to less than an inch long, and as big as the saltwater crocodile, which can grow to more than 17 feet in length and weigh more than 3,000 pounds.

Is It Just the Scales?

Like other members of the animal kingdom, all reptiles have certain special traits that make them a part of their own family of animals. In reptiles, the two most important traits are that they are all cold-blooded and that they are all covered in scales.

Since a reptile is cold-blooded, its body temperature adjusts to its surroundings. That means that when a reptile gets too hot, it must move to water or shade to cool itself off. And if it gets too cold, it has to move to a sunny place to warm itself up.

This close-up of a python shows the many small scales that cover a snake's body. This snake is from the Pacific island nation of New Guinea.

One of the myths about reptiles, especially snakes, is that they are slimy to the touch. Actually, since all reptiles have scales, they are anything but slimy. The skins of some reptiles are very smooth because they are covered with very small scales. Some reptile skins are used to make people's clothing and shoes.

Most reptiles reproduce by laying eggs, but a few kinds give birth to live young. All turtles, tortoises, crocodiles, and alligators lay eggs. So do most lizards. All boas, vipers, and garter snakes give birth to live babies. So do a few species of lizards called *skinks*.

Most reptiles lay their eggs or give birth to their young, then leave them on their own. A few kinds of reptiles protect their eggs until they hatch. Alligators and crocodiles are known for guarding their nests and for helping their babies emerge from their eggs. Female pythons are known for coiling their bodies around their eggs to give them protection from predators and to keep them at the right temperature.

The skink (not skunk) eats mainly bugs— like crickets, grasshoppers, and beetles.

The eastern milk snake is a colorful species found in North America and South America. It got its name because in the past people believed they often went into barns and sucked milk from dairy cows. Of course, this story wasn't true. Actually, snakes don't drink milk at all! Milk snakes are actually beneficial to farmers because they help keep the population of rodents, which they eat, in check. Although milk snakes look a lot like the poisonous coral snake, they aren't venomous.

The Reptile Family Tree

All reptiles have backbones, and that means they are all vertebrates from the phylum *Chordata*. There is only one class of reptiles, which scientists refer to as *Reptilia*.

Why are they called snapping turtles? Because they can snap at you with those sharp beaks!

Scientists have placed reptiles that live on Earth today in four orders and a few suborders. The largest order of reptiles (about 7,900 species) is *Squamata*. This order includes lizards, snakes, and creatures in the family *Amphisbaenids* (better known as worm lizards). The second biggest order of reptiles (300 species) is *Testudines*. It includes the shelled reptiles—turtles, tortoises, and terrapins. The order *Crocodilia* includes 23 species of crocodiles, alligators, gavials, and caimans. The order *Sphenodontia* includes just two lizard-like species that live in New Zealand.

The orders of reptiles are broken into families and subfamilies. The order Squamata, for example, includes about 20 different families of lizards and about 18 different families of snakes. Each of these families is broken down into different genera, and each genus includes a certain number of species.

There are almost 5,000 species of lizards living in the world today, making them the most common of reptile species. Second among the reptiles as far as the number of species is concerned is snakes. There are about 2,700 different kinds of snakes; only 375 of them are poisonous.

That's a poisonous rattlesnake, looking threatening!

The Mystery of the Dinosaurs

The biggest reptiles ever to live on Earth were the dinosaurs. All dinosaurs are extinct now. That means that they no longer live on Earth. No one knows for sure why all the dinosaurs became extinct. What scientists *do* know is that there were many kinds of dinosaurs in many shapes and sizes. They know that because they have found many dinosaur bones that were left behind when the dinosaurs died out.

Did you know that the name *dinosaur* came from an old Greek word that means "terrible lizard"? Actually, dinosaurs weren't really lizards, even though they were reptiles. Most of them weren't so terrible, either. Most dinosaurs were really big reptiles that ate plants. But some of the dinosaurs, like the tyrannosaurs, ate meat.

For a long time, the brachiosaur was thought to be the largest dinosaur. Many scientists believe the brachiosaur grew up to 82 feet long, but some believe they could have been even bigger.

The brachiosaur had a long neck like a giraffe, and scientists believe it could raise its head more than 40 feet above the ground. But scientists believe there were dinosaurs even bigger than the brachiosaur. Bones from an enormous dinosaur called *Argentinosaurus* were recently discovered in South America. Scientists believe this dinosaur could have

grown to over 100 feet long and weighed over 100 tons. Another dinosaur, called *Sauroposeidon*, was recently discovered that may have been heavier than the brachiosaur.

Different people believe different things about where dinosaurs fit in with the creation story in Genesis 1. Some believe that God created everything in six actual 24-hour days, and that the earth is between 6,000 and 10,000 years old. That would mean that dinosaurs and people lived at the same time. Other people believe that the six days God used to create the world and all life on it weren't really actual days. Instead, they believe that these "days" were really long periods of time with gaps in between them. They believe that the earth is millions or billions of years old and that dinosaurs had become extinct a long time before God created humans.

Some people even believe that dinosaurs are mentioned in the Bible. They point to names in scripture like *leviathan, behemoth, sea serpent,* and *dragon.* But the Bible doesn't say anything at all about what happened to the dinosaurs—or any other of the many creatures that at one time lived on Earth but are now extinct.

Amphibians: Animals That Live Two Lives

There are more than 6,000 species of amphibians living on Earth today. That includes frogs, toads, salamanders, newts, and strange creatures called *caecilians* (tropical amphibians that look like snakes or worms at a glance because they have no legs and a very short tail).

Some amphibians are among the strangest animals on Earth. For example, the Chinese giant (and we mean *giant!*) salamander is the world's biggest amphibian, growing up to almost six feet long. Then there's the olm, a blind salamander with transparent skin that lives in water that flows underground and can survive without food for ten years. And there is also the lungless salamander of Mexico, a species that doesn't have lungs but takes in oxygen through its skin and mouth lining.

All amphibians are vertebrates that belong to the class of animals called *Amphibia. Amphibia* is a Greek word that means "two lives." That's because amphibians spend their lives in two places: in water and on land.

Amphibians that live on Earth today all belong to the subclass of animals called *Lissamphibia.* This subclass includes the orders *Anura* (frogs and toads), *Caudata* (salamanders and newts), and *Apoda* (caecilians). These orders are broken down into families, with the families broken down into genera. Each genus includes one or more individual species.

Amphibians: Kind of Like Reptiles. . .but Different

Amphibians are a lot like reptiles in some ways. Both are cold-blooded vertebrates that can be found all over the world. And most kinds of reptiles and amphibians reproduce by laying eggs. But amphibians are also a lot different from reptiles in some very important areas.

The most important way amphibians are different from reptiles is in how they reproduce. Reptile eggs have hard, leathery shells that are designed to protect the developing babies living inside. Many reptiles lay their eggs in well-hidden nests that are protected from hot or cold weather. Amphibians, on the other hand, lay soft eggs that don't have a protective shell. They usually attach the eggs to the stems of plants growing in the water. If you were to look around pond plants during the mating season of amphibians, you would likely find clear blobs of goo with tiny frog or salamander eggs inside them.

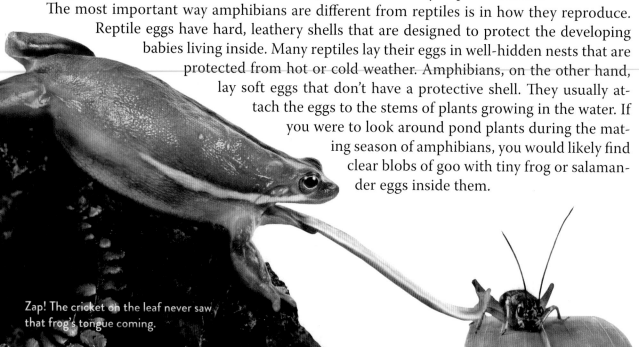

Zap! The cricket on the leaf never saw that frog's tongue coming.

Most newly hatched reptiles look pretty much like the adults of the species. But most amphibians begin their lives in water and look nothing like their parents. This is called the *tadpole stage* of the amphibian's life. During that stage, the amphibian looks and acts more like a fish than an amphibian. It has fins and a tail and breathes using gills. Most of the time, it doesn't have legs. Most tadpoles feed on plants and algae they find in the water, but some feed on smaller tadpoles and other animals that live in water.

As the tadpole begins growing into an adult amphibian, it loses its gills as it develops lungs and forms legs so that it can begin its life on land. During that time, its mouth will also grow into the same width as its head, preparing it for feeding on what full-grown amphibians eat.

THAT'S WEIRD!

A Betic midwife toad is actually a species of frog that lives in Spain. These frogs are known for two weird things. First, they have warts on their backs that give off a strong-smelling poison when they are attacked or scared. Second, after mating, the female lays strings of fertilized eggs, which the male carries around his hind legs until they are ready to hatch. When it is time for the tadpoles to emerge from the eggs, the male deposits them in the water, where they begin the process of maturing into baby Betic midwife toads.

A frog sits in the water, surrounded by its eggs (also called *spawn*).

Arthropods: Creation's Creepy Crawlers and Flyers

Can you remember the last time you came face-to-face with a kind of animal called an *arthropod*? If you're not so sure when you have, then there are a few things about arthropods you need to know.

First of all, there are millions of species of arthropods. Second, arthropods live all over the world—in salt water, in fresh water, on land, in the air, and in the soil. Between 80 and 85 percent of animal species alive on Earth today are arthropods.

If you're still not so sure when the last time was that you saw an arthropod, then consider this: all insects are arthropods. So if you've seen an ant, a housefly, a bee, or a butterfly today, you've seen an arthropod.

Insects aren't the only animals scientists classify as arthropods. Spiders, centipedes, mites, ticks, lobsters, crabs, crayfish, scorpions, and many other animals are also arthropods—and they are all important parts in God's perfect plan of creation.

Spiders weave a web of silk to catch other spiders and bugs as food. Some large spiders can catch and eat small birds and lizards!

What Is an Arthropod?

Arthropods all share certain traits that make them arthropods. First of all, arthropods are all invertebrates. Other animals you have already read about in this book—fish, birds, mammals, reptiles, and amphibians—are vertebrates, which means they have backbones. An invertebrate, on the other hand, is an animal that has no backbone.

Instead of a backbone, or any other bones, arthropods have what *entomologists*—scientists who study insects—call an *exoskeleton*. An exoskeleton is basically a hard shell on the outside of the body that acts like a coat of armor. The exoskeleton pro-

Most millipedes eat dead leaves and live between one and ten years.

tects the arthropod from predators and other outside dangers. An arthropod's exoskeleton is soft when it is first born, but it hardens as the animal matures. Many young arthropods shed their exoskeletons and grow new ones as they get bigger.

Arthropod is a Greek word that mixes the words *joint* and *foot*. This means that any animal that has more than four jointed legs is an arthropod. That includes all insects, spiders, centipedes, crustaceans (like crabs and lobsters), and a long, long list of other animals. Spiders, crabs, and other species of arthropods have eight legs. Centipedes and millipedes can have anywhere from 30 to hundreds of legs.

Arthropods are also known for their *segmented bodies*. That means that their bodies are made up of more than one part. Flies and other insects have three body segments, while spiders have two. Most millipedes have 30 to 40 body segments.

Like fish, reptiles, and amphibians, arthropods are cold-blooded animals. Remember, the body temperature of all cold-blooded animals depends on the temperature of the water or air that surrounds them.

The Arthropod Family Tree

Scientists believe there are between four and six million species of arthropods living in the world today. That is more species than the rest of the animal kingdom combined! All arthropods belong to the phylum of animals called *Arthropoda*.

Scientists have placed all known arthropods into 11 different classes of animals. The class with the most known kinds of animals is called *Insecta*—you guessed it—insects! Even though scientists have identified and named just over one million species of insects, they believe there could be between six and ten million species living in the world today.

Insects all have the hard outer skeletons all arthropods have. They also have a three-part body (head, thorax, and abdomen) and three pairs of jointed legs. Insects also have what are called *compound eyes*.

Flies—like this common housefly—have large "compound eyes" made up of thousands of round lenses.

Compound eyes have many different lenses to see out of, instead of just one like human eyes have. Insects also have two antennae. Ants, bees, beetles, butterflies, moths, grasshoppers, and dragonflies are all insects, and there are thousands to hundreds of thousands of species of each of them.

A ruby tiger moth shows off its antennae (in white).

Another large class of arthropods that live on land is called *Arachnida*. These animals are more commonly called *arachnids*. Spiders, ticks, mites, and scorpions are all arachnids. All arachnids have eight legs—even though some arachnids' front legs are designed as claws. The best-known arachnids are spiders. There are about 38,000 known species of spiders living in the world today.

The Importance of Arthropods

Many arthropods are creepy, crawly creatures, and some of them are kind of scary looking. Most people consider some arthropods—like houseflies or grasshoppers—pests.

But, hey, even if they are a little on the scary or ugly side, and even if they are capable of causing people trouble, they're also creations of God—and they are important to humans and other animals for many different reasons.

Many species of fish, birds, and mammals often eat arthropods, and some of them eat *only* arthropods. Krill, which are shrimplike arthropods that live in the ocean, are an important part of many sea animals' diets. Many freshwater fish eat mostly insects and krill larvae. And as you read in chapter 6, some birds are specially equipped with beaks that make it easy for them to catch insects to eat.

This krill looks something like the shrimp you might eat at a seafood restaurant.

Some crustaceans, which are all arthropods, are important parts of the human diet in many parts of the world. Crabs, lobsters, crayfish, shrimps, and prawns are all popular for food all over the world. In some cultures, insects and their *grubs* (larvae) are eaten raw and cooked. Believe it or not, tarantulas are considered a delicacy in some parts of the world!

Yes, that's a plate of cooked tarantulas. They're a snack in the Asian nation of Cambodia.

The arthropod that plays the most important part in supplying food to humans around the world is the bee. That's not just because many people like to eat honey. Bees help in *pollination*, which is a process absolutely necessary in the production of many fruits and vegetables. Pollination happens when pollen is transferred from one plant to another plant of the same species. That process allows plants to reproduce and bear fruit.

Many arthropods are important to humans because they help control populations of pests that destroy crops. Spiders and scorpions eat insects that eat plant life, including plants that produce food for humans. Ladybugs are even important this way because they eat aphids, tiny plant-eating insects that can make short work of a vegetable garden if they aren't controlled.

EXPLORING THE WORLD OF LAND ANIMALS

What kind of land animals do you find most interesting? Mammals? Reptiles? Amphibians? Arthropods? Take the time to learn about the kind of animal that is most interesting to you. Read about those animals, or visit a city zoo, wildlife center, or other place where you can see the animals in person. As you read and observe, ask yourself these questions: How are these animals different from other types of land animals? How are they like other land animals? What do they eat? Where do they live in the wild? How do they benefit humans? Maybe you can use what you learn in a school report, but maybe you'll just have fun learning about the animals you think are most interesting!

One Final Step to Go!

God spent most of two days creating the millions of animals that live in the water and on dry ground—and some that split their time in both places. He made animals that swim, animals that fly, animals that walk, animals that crawl, animals that burrow, and animals that just stay in one place most of their lives.

You probably wonder why God made many of the animals He did. Some of them don't seem to have any real purpose other than just being what they are. But every animal God made had its own special place in His wonderful plan of creation. Every animal would become part of a kingdom that would feed itself and reproduce itself until the end of time.

But God wasn't finished. Now that He had created everything you can see—and some things you can't—it was time for Him to finish His work of creation by making the one being He did it all for in the first place. That means you!

CHAPTER 8

DAY 6, PART II
HUMANS: MADE IN GOD'S IMAGE

Then God said, "Let us make human beings in our image, to be like us. They will reign over the fish in the sea, the birds in the sky, the livestock, all the wild animals on the earth, and the small animals that scurry along the ground." So God created human beings in his own image. In the image of God he created them; male and female he created them. Then God blessed them and said, "Be fruitful and multiply. Fill the earth and govern it. Reign over the fish in the sea, the birds in the sky, and all the animals that scurry along the ground."

GENESIS 1:26–28

After working more than five days to create the universe, the earth, and everything that lives on Earth, God did something very different from what He had been doing. The Bible tells us that when He created us humans, it was the first time He made something "in his own image" (Genesis 1:27).

You can see a lot of what God is like in everything He created. When you look outside Earth and see the stars, planets, galaxies, and other things He placed in outer space, you can see just how big and powerful He is. When you look at the earth and how it is put together, you can see that God pays close attention to the details and that He made sure that every living thing He later created would be cared for. And when you look at the amazing number of plants and animals and other living things on Earth now, you can see that God is very creative and really likes variety.

But none of those things—as amazing and wonderful as they are—are made in God's own image like we humans are.

What Sets You Apart from Animals

What do you think it means that we humans are created in God's own image? Actually, it means a lot of things.

Dolphins raise their tails at a trainer's command—and receive a treat in return.

It doesn't mean that God has a physical body like you do. It also doesn't mean that you have the power God has, to create something out of nothing. But God created us humans to rule over the world and over all the animals that live here with us.

God made some animals to be a lot like us humans in some ways. For example, some of the world's most intelligent animals—such as primates, some water mammals (like dolphins, which are known for their amazing intelligence), and others—seem to have the ability to use their brains in ways very much like you use yours. In other words, they're just plain smarter than most animals. And some animals are very sociable, which means they live and travel in tightly knit families.

But God made people different from animals—and like Himself—in many important ways. First of all, we're made different from animals in how we think and reason. Even the most intelligent animals on Earth aren't able to use their brains the way we humans can. For example, only humans are able to read and understand the Bible and other written materials. And no animal is able to solve a complicated math equation or to figure out how to take apart and reassemble things like puzzles or car engines.

God also gave us humans the gift of creativity. Even though humans can't create on the same scale as God has, we all have the ability to use our minds and hands to create all sorts of new things—like art, music, technology, and other important human creations.

God also made us like Him in the way we communicate, both with God and with one another. While some animals have the ability to communicate using different sounds, none of them has the ability to use words like we can. God began creation with the simple words *"Let there be. . ."* , and it was so.

You can dress up a monkey, but you can't make her human!

From tiny computer chips to massive skyscrapers, the creativity of human beings is unmatched in the animal world.

God made us humans different from animals in that we can know the difference between good and evil and right and wrong. He also gave us the free will to choose right and wrong. Adam and Eve, the very first humans in all creation, were given the choice between right and wrong. Sadly, they chose to do the wrong thing—the one and only thing God told them *not* to do. But even though Adam and Eve messed up, we humans still reflect the image of God because we can choose to do what is right in His eyes.

Adam and Eve are kicked out of the garden of Eden for disobeying God.

The most important way God made us humans different from animals is that we have an awareness of our Creator. Not only that, but we have the ability to communicate and fellowship with Him. God also gave each of us an eternal soul, the part of us that lives on after our bodies die. And God has lovingly given us the opportunity to be with Him forever after we die.

Your Body—God's Most Amazing Creation

Before God created us humans, He put together an amazing universe and planet Earth. He created billions of galaxies, each of which contains billions of stars. He created our solar system and designed it perfectly so that our earth could support us and millions of other living things that make their home here.

But as awesome as all these creations are, they've got nothing on the human body. Your body is the most incredible, complicated living thing in the whole world. God designed your body with many different *systems* that all work together perfectly to keep you moving, thinking, talking, and growing.

These different systems include your

If you could see inside yourself, you'd look something like this. Aren't you glad you have skin?

- nervous system (your brain, spinal cord, and nerves);
- cardiovascular system (your heart, blood, and vessels);
- lymphatic/immune system (your lymph and lymph nodes and white blood cells);
- respiratory system (your nose, trachea, and lungs);
- digestive system (your mouth, esophagus, stomach, and intestines);
- muscular system (your muscles and tendons);
- skeletal system (your bones);
- dermal system (your hair, skin, and nails);
- excretory system (your lungs, large intestine, kidneys, and skin);
- endocrine system (your glands);
- reproductive system (your reproductive organs).

All these systems—and a few others—together make up your entire body. And by the time you are fully grown, they will account for about 100 trillion individual cells, 206 bones, 600 muscles, and 22 internal organs.

DID YOU KNOW. . . ?

There are a total of 206 bones in the bodies of adult human beings (more than half of which are in the hands and feet), but between 300 and 350 bones in the body of a baby. That's because some of the bones of babies fuse together as they grow. There are four classes of bones in the human body. There are the *long bones*, which make up the limbs. There are the *short bones*, which are grouped together to strengthen your skeleton. There are the *flat bones*, which protect your body and provide a place for the muscles to attach. Finally, there are the *irregular bones*, oddly shaped bones that don't fit into the other three classes.

No wonder that thousands of years ago, a man named David—the greatest king the nation of Israel ever had and the man who wrote many of the Old Testament psalms—declared his amazement at the design of his own body when he wrote, "You made all the delicate, inner parts of my body and knit me together in my mother's womb. Thank you for making me so wonderfully complex! Your workmanship is marvelous—how well I know it" (Psalm 139:13–14).

How We've Learned about the Human Body

One of the most important ways humans have used their God-given capacity for creativity and thought is in the study of the human body and medicine. We humans have always had a curiosity about how our bodies work, as well as a need to understand how to diagnose and treat people who are sick or injured. Over the past century, what we know about the human body has grown incredibly. So have the technology and knowledge doctors use to help people who are sick or injured.

A doctor reviews a chest X-ray.

The technology scientists and doctors use on the human body is nothing more than the harnessing of what God has already created and using it in medicine. For example, the sun and other stars give off X-rays, which are used in medicine today. X-rays have also been called *Roentgen rays*, after Wilhelm Konrad Roentgen, the German scientist who discovered them and developed ways to use them in medicine. Doctors use X-rays to see images from inside the body, such as the skeleton, and also in *angiograms* (picture images of the blood vessels).

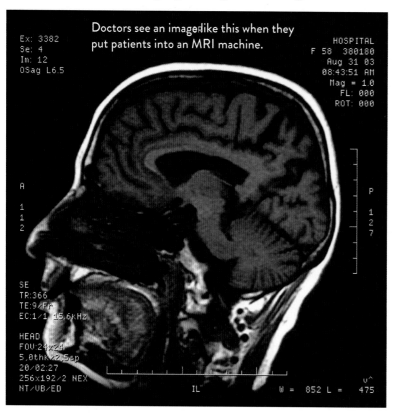

Doctors see an image like this when they put patients into an MRI machine.

Ex: 3382
Se: 4
Im: 12
OSag L6.5

HOSPITAL
F 58   380180
Aug 31 03
08:43:51 AM
Mag = 1.0
FL: 000
ROT: 000

A

P

1
1
2

1
2
7

SE
TR:366
TE:9/Fr
EC:1/1 15.6kHz

HEAD
FOV:24x24
5.0thk/2.5sp
20/02:27
256x192/2 NEX
NT/VB/ED

IL

W = 852 L = 475

While an X-ray gives doctors a *two-dimensional* (flat, like the pages of a book) look at some parts of the human body, a Computed Axial Tomography scan (or CAT scan) allows doctors to have a *three-dimensional* (height, width, and depth) look inside the human body. A CAT scan of the brain or other organs gives a lot more information than a regular X-ray. The CAT scan can allow a brain specialist to look at "slices" of the brain, which helps make finding tumors and other problems easier.

Magnetic Resonance Imaging (MRI) is a form of medical technology that gives detailed pictures of internal body parts. Unlike the X-ray or the CAT scan, the MRI doesn't use radiation or other radioactive substances of any kind. Instead, the patient is placed in a magnetic field while radio waves, which are completely harmless to the human body, are turned on and off. The body then emits its own weak radio signals, which are picked up by an antenna and fed to a computer. This produces detailed images of what is going on inside the body.

THE WAY IT USED TO BE

Today, if you were to get really sick, you would go to a doctor who would figure out what is wrong with you and then give you the medicine you need to get well. But there was a time when doctors used leeches—little creatures that look kinda like slugs and feed on blood—to treat their patients. Up until about the mid-1800s, it was believed that people got sick because of imbalances in their bodies and that one of the best ways to get rid of those imbalances was to allow leeches to take out the "bad blood" that caused those imbalances and made people sick. This procedure was called *bloodletting*.

A Perfectly Designed "Control Center"

You probably haven't given a lot of thought about just how your family's car works—other than it needs fuel to take you and your family where you need to go. But today's car engines are designed to operate best through a small computer inside the dashboard that acts as a control center that keeps everything in working order.

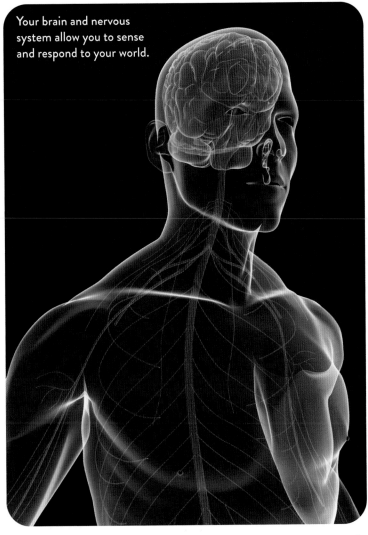

Your brain and nervous system allow you to sense and respond to your world.

God designed your body with a "control center" of its own that keeps every part of your body working the way He meant it to work. It's called your *brain*, and it is the key part of what is called your *nervous system*.

Your nervous system is made up of the brain, the spinal cord, and a huge arrangement of nerves that starts at the top of your head and goes all the way to the bottom of your feet. Your brain weighs about three pounds, and it sends messages to and receives messages from about 45 miles of nerves that run through your entire body.

Your brain is the most amazing organ in your whole body. You use your brain to store different kinds of information—like people and facts you know, things you need to remember, and what you need to do at certain times and in certain situations. You also use your brain to do things you choose to do—like eating, walking, reading, and playing ball. And, of course, you use your brain for thinking!

DID YOU KNOW. . . ?

If you've ever been to a meat market and seen calves' brains—yes, believe it or not, some people like to eat calves' brains—then you have a general idea what your own brain looks like. Your brain will never take first place in a beauty contest. In fact, it looks kinda gross! But of all the things God created, there are few more amazing than that three-pound organ He put between your ears. Your brain is made up of more than ten billion nerve cells and more than 50 billion other cells.

Your brain also controls every other function of your body, including the things you don't have to think about doing. You breathe because your brain tells your lungs to take in air. Your heart beats because your brain sends it signals telling it to pump blood throughout your body. And your digestive system does what it needs to do because your brain tells your mouth, your stomach, your intestines, and other parts of your digestive system what to do and when to do it.

Your brain is made up of five parts: the cerebrum, the cerebellum, the brain stem, the pituitary gland, and the hypothalamus. Each of these parts plays a vital role in how your mind and body function. The *cerebrum* is the largest part of your brain. It is the part you use for thinking, memory, and voluntary muscle movements. The *cerebellum* is the part of the brain that controls your balance, movement, and coordination. Without your cerebellum doing its work, you couldn't walk, stand, or move around.

Your Cardiovascular System

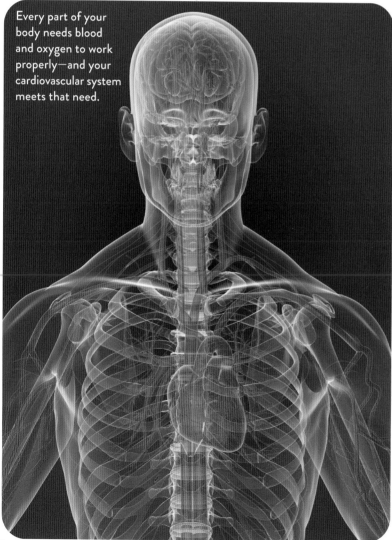

Every part of your body needs blood and oxygen to work properly—and your cardiovascular system meets that need.

If you think your nervous system is the most incredible part of your body, then you might find the *cardiovascular system*—which consists of your heart, blood, and blood vessels—a close second.

Your heart is the single largest part of your cardiovascular system. Your heart's job is to pump blood through your body. The heart of an average grownup human beats just a little under 104,000 times a day, while a child's heart beats about 129,000 to 172,000 times a day. As the heart beats, it pumps blood through your body so that it can provide your body with the nutrients and oxygen it needs.

Your body contains an amazing 60,000 miles of *blood vessels*, which are tubes that carry blood from one part of the body to another. There are three kinds of blood vessels in your body. There are the *arteries*, which carry blood away from your heart.

If you were a blood cell, this is what you'd see as you left the heart for other parts of the body.

There are the *veins*, which take blood back to your heart. And there are the *capillaries*, which are tiny vessels that supply your entire body with oxygen and other nutrients. The capillaries are the smallest blood vessels. Most of them are so small that blood cells have to line up single file just to pass through them.

EXPLORING THE HUMAN BODY

If you want to learn more about how your body works, you can find mountains of information in your school library and on the internet. A good way to do your study is to investigate the systems in the human body one by one. Here they are: the circulatory system, the dermal system, the digestive system, the endocrine system, the excretory system, the lymphatic/immune system, the muscular system, the nervous system, the reproductive system, the respiratory system, and the skeletal system.

Your Respiratory System

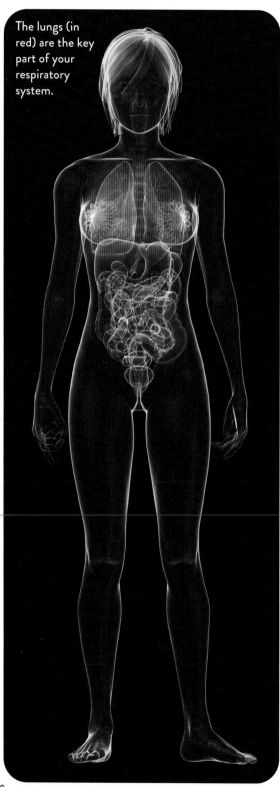

The lungs (in red) are the key part of your respiratory system.

Have you ever had a contest with your friends to see who could hold their breath the longest? If you have, then you know that it's not more than a few seconds after you stop breathing that you really want to take a breath again. That's because it's only a matter of a few seconds before your body realizes you've stopped taking in oxygen and starts screaming at your brain, *I need oxygen!*

Oxygen is one of the elements your body needs to survive. The cells in your body use oxygen to perform every one of the basic functions of life—walking, running, thinking, eating, sitting still—even sleeping! When the cells in your body use oxygen, they produce a gas called *carbon dioxide.* Even though there is always carbon dioxide in your body, too much of it can make a person sick or even die.

This is where your *respiratory system* comes in.

Your respiratory system serves one simple purpose: to bring oxygen into your body and to remove carbon dioxide from your body. Your lungs are the biggest and most important part of your respiratory system. They work closely with your circulatory system to bring oxygen to your cells and to remove the poisonous carbon dioxide.

Here's how it works.

When you breathe in, you fill your lungs with fresh, oxygen-filled air. At the same time, your heart pumps blood into the walls of your lungs through your blood vessels. When the blood reaches the walls of your lungs, it releases carbon dioxide into your lungs and absorbs oxygen and takes it to the rest of your body. After the oxygen-rich blood leaves your lungs, it goes back to your heart, which pumps it out through your body. When you breathe out, you release the carbon dioxide into the air around you.

Have you ever wondered why your heart beats faster and you breathe harder when you're exercising—playing basketball with your friends, hiking with your family, or running in gym class? It's because when you exercise, your body uses a lot more oxygen than it does when you're sitting still. Your lungs and heart always work together to take in the oxygen you need and then deliver it to your muscles and other parts of your body to work right, but they have to work harder when your muscles send the signal, *I need more oxygen!* So you end up breathing harder.

What Happens When You Eat—Digestion!

Can you remember the last time you started to feel hungry? Maybe it was almost lunchtime at school, and you began to feel your stomach growl—and maybe hear a few of your classmates'

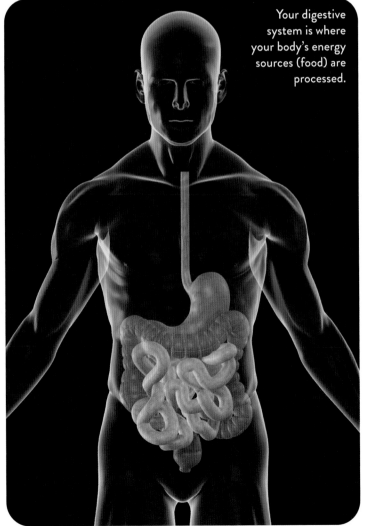

Your digestive system is where your body's energy sources (food) are processed.

stomachs doing the same thing.

As lunchtime grew closer and you began to think about eating, your mouth might have started to water a little bit. And if you started to smell the food you were about to have for lunch, your stomach growled louder and your mouth watered even more. It seemed like all you could think about was a delicious slice of pizza or that turkey sandwich you brought to school with you for lunch.

This doesn't happen just because you like food. It's your body telling you it's time to eat!

Like all living things, you need food to survive. Food is the source of the energy you need to get through the day as well as the vitamins and other essential nutrients your body needs to grow, develop, heal, and function in every other way.

Your *digestive system* is an amazing system of organs that allows your body to convert food into energy. It includes your mouth, your esophagus, your stomach, and your large and small intestines. That slice of pizza or turkey sandwich wouldn't do your body a bit of good if it wasn't digested, but every part of your digestive system works together to convert the things you eat into energy and nutrients your body can use to keep it running well.

Digestion starts with the part you enjoy the most: eating! When you take a bite of food, your teeth begin crushing it into pieces small enough to swallow—and small enough for your stomach to begin breaking down. At that same time, glands in your mouth and throat produce *saliva* (you might know it better as spit), which moistens your food to make it easier to swallow and which begins breaking down your food.

After you swallow your food, it travels down your *esophagus*. The esophagus is a long, slippery tube that goes from your throat to your stomach. It has muscles inside it that force food down toward the stomach.

Your stomach has muscles it uses to grind and mix the food you have eaten. It also has glands that release the chemicals hydrochloric acid and pepsin, which together break the food down into a goopy mixture called *chyme*. The chyme then moves into your small intestine, where several chemicals break down the food even more. At that same time, your liver adds a liquid substance called *bile*, which helps neutralize the acids from your stomach. That helps move the process of digestion along.

As the chyme slowly moves along in your small intestine—aided by muscles that squeeze and roll it—the process of digestion is almost complete. Inside your small intestine, tiny folds called *villi* absorb all the nutrients from the chyme. What is left is the waste material your body can't use. Those materials enter your large intestine, which helps rid you of the leftover waste.

THAT'S WEIRD!

When you hear the word *bacteria*, you probably think of those little bugs that can make you sick. But there are lots of different kinds of bacteria in your body. Some of them can make you sick, and others are just there not really doing anything. But several kinds of bacteria working in your body help keep you healthy. Believe it or not, your body needs bacteria just to survive! Some of the good bacteria in your body help with digestion of food, with the breaking down of waste products, with cleaning out the bad stuff from your intestines, and with producing vitamins and other nutrients your body needs.

You've Got Muscles!

Remember the last time you saw a super bulked-up bodybuilder? You probably thought to yourself, *Wow! He's really got muscles!* Actually, you have the same number of muscles as even the beefiest-looking bodybuilder in the world. It's just that a bodybuilder spends a lot of time developing his muscles at the gym and making them bigger.

Any time you move, you're using one or more of the muscles your body is designed to have. You use muscles when you run, jump, throw a ball, or pick up a book. You even use your muscles when you smile or blink your eyes.

On average, about 40 percent of a human's body weight is muscle. Your body includes large muscles, like the ones in your legs, to very tiny muscles, like the ones you are using to read this book (yes, your eyes move back and forth because of tiny muscles attached to them). Each muscle in your body is designed to do different kinds of work.

Your body includes three different kinds of muscles: skeletal muscles, smooth muscles, and cardiac muscles. Most of your *skeletal muscles* are attached to your bones with strong, flexible strands of tissue called *tendons*. These muscles are used in voluntary movements like raising your arms or scratching your leg. The largest muscles in your body are skeletal muscles.

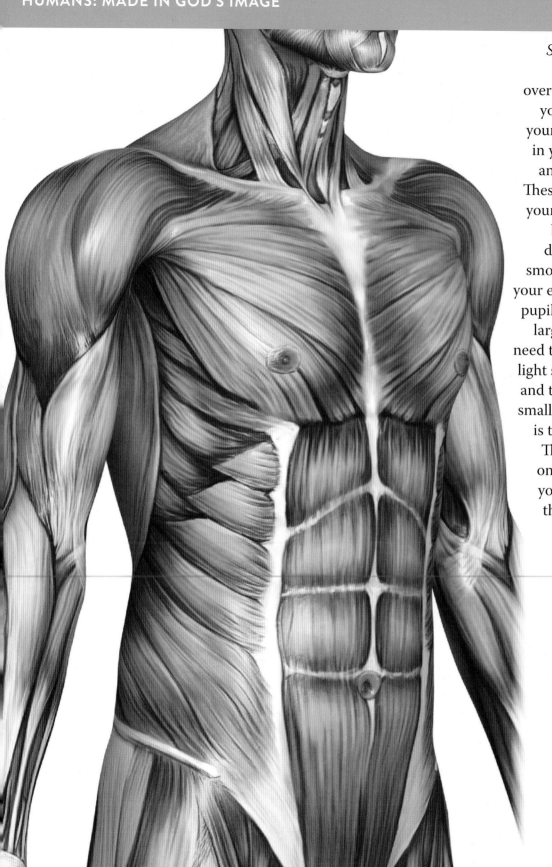

Smooth muscles are found all over your body—in your stomach, in your blood vessels, in your intestines, and in your eyes. These muscles help your body regulate blood flow and digest food. The smooth muscles in your eyes cause your pupils to *dilate* (get larger) when they need to take in more light so you can see, and to *contract* (get smaller) when there is too much light. There is actually only one place in your whole body that has *cardiac muscles*: your heart! Your heart is a big, strong muscle that beats even when you're not thinking about it.

Your Inner Frame: The Skeletal System

Have you ever gone by a building site and seen how a house is constructed? After the foundation is laid, builders assemble the house's frame—the part that will both support the rest of the house and give the builders something to build on as they work to make the house ready for people to live in.

In a way, your body is constructed very much like a house. But instead of a frame made of wood, you have one made of strong material that forms your skeleton. Without your skeleton, you couldn't run, walk, or stand upright.

Your skeleton is made up of four main types of bones. You have *long bones* in your arms and legs and *short bones* in your hands, feet, and spine. You also have *flat bones* to protect your organs. Finally, you have what are called *irregular bones*, which are bones that don't fit in with the other three types.

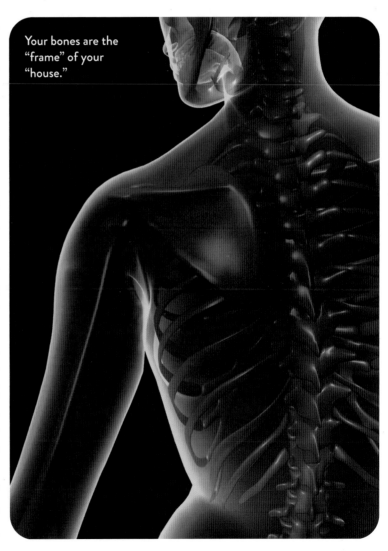

Your bones are the "frame" of your "house."

Your bones are strong enough to support your weight, hold you upright, and protect your organs, but they are also light enough to allow you to walk, run, and jump. If your bones were any weaker, they would break easily in even the lightest movement, but if they were any heavier, they would make it difficult to move around as freely and quickly as you do.

More than half of the bones in your whole body are found in your hands and feet. These bones, along with the ligaments and tendons in your hands, give your hands the flexibility they need to do things like grasp a pencil or pen or play a musical instrument. And they give your feet the flexibility they need to help you keep your balance when you walk or run.

Your bones also serve one other very important purpose. Not only do they give you strength and support and protect your internal organs, but they also produce new blood for your entire body. Your blood is made up of millions and millions of microscopic cells that live for only a few months. That means they have to be regularly replaced. In the center of your bones is a spongy material called *marrow*. The marrow is the part of your bones that creates new blood cells to replace the old ones that die or the ones you lose when you bleed.

RECORD BREAKING

Two men pose by a full-size statue of Robert Wadlow, outside the Guinness World Records Museum in Copenhagen, Denmark.

The tallest man in medical history was Robert Wadlow, who measured an amazing 8 feet, 11 inches tall at the time of his death in 1940. Wadlow weighed 490 pounds at the end of his life. He was known as the "Alton Giant," after his hometown of Alton, Illinois. The world's all-time tallest woman was Zeng Jinlian, who reached a height of 8 feet, 1¾ inches before she died in 1982 at the age of 17. Zeng Jinlian was the only woman among 12 people in medical history who grew to over 8 feet tall.

Here are some interesting—and really weird—facts about your skin. First, your skin is the largest organ in your whole body, with a surface area of about 21 square feet. Second, humans shed about 600,000 tiny particles of skin every hour, which accounts for about 1.5 pounds of skin a year and about 105 pounds in a lifetime for someone who reaches 70 years of age. Third, humans shed and regrow their outer skin cells about every 27 days. Finally (and this is *really* weird—and gross), most dust particles in your house are made of dead skin.

The color might vary from person to person, but our skin is always working for us!

Other Important Systems

In addition to the ones listed earlier, your body has several other important systems that work to keep your body operating and growing.

Your *integumentary system* includes the heaviest organ you have—your skin. Your skin serves a lot of important purposes. It is designed to protect your body from germs and viruses that can cause you to become sick. It also keeps your body from losing too much water and dehydrating and insulates your body and helps keep it from overheating or from cooling off too much. Finally, your skin actually produces vitamin D when it is exposed to sunlight.

Your *lymphatic/immune system* helps protect you from bad bacteria that could cause you to become ill. This system includes your lymph and lymph nodes as well as your white blood cells. Your lymph nodes produce immune cells that help the body fight infection. Your white blood cells—which are also called *leukocytes*—help defend your body against infections by feasting on bacteria and other dangerous organisms and materials that make their way into your body.

Your *excretory system* serves to rid your body of wastes and toxins that build up as a result of other bodily functions. Your lungs are part of your respiratory system, but they are also part of your excretory system because they help rid your body of the carbon dioxide your blood cells carry back from cells that have processed oxygen. Your large and small intestines are part of your digestive system, but they are also part of your excretory system because they help rid your body of waste that is left over after your body has fully digested the food you eat. And your kidneys work day and night to clean the waste and toxins out of your blood.

Your *endocrine system* is a bunch of glands that serve some very important purposes in your body. *Glands* are organs that release different kinds of chemicals called *hormones* into your body. You have more than 30 different hormones working in your body to cause all kinds of things to happen. Hormones regulate your body temperature, control your growth and physical maturity, and even help you to feel hungry when your body knows it's time to eat. They even help you to handle stressful or frightening situations you may face.

When God created us humans, He made us "male and female" (Genesis 1:27). That is so we could follow His command to "be fruitful and multiply. Fill the earth and govern it. Reign over the fish in the sea, the birds in the sky, and all the animals that scurry along the ground" (Genesis 1:28).

God made all men and women (and boys and girls) in His own image, but He also made them very different in some very important ways. He equipped women with the internal organs they would need in order to give birth to children, and He equipped men with the organs they would need to father children. These organs are all part of humankind's *reproductive system*.

CHAPTER 9

DAY 6, PART III:
CREATION COMPLETE. . .NOW WHAT?

Then God said, "Look! I have given you every seed-bearing plant throughout the earth and all the fruit trees for your food. And I have given every green plant as food for all the wild animals, the birds in the sky, and the small animals that scurry along the ground—everything that has life." And that is what happened. Then God looked over all he had made, and he saw that it was very good! And evening passed and morning came, marking the sixth day.

GENESIS 1:29–31

CREATION COMPLETE. . .NOW WHAT?

If you were to go back and read the first chapter of Genesis and take a count of the times God looked at something He had created and said it was "good," you'd find that word used six different times in that part of the Bible. But as the sixth and final day of creation—the day He created us humans—drew to a close, God looked at everything He had created and saw that it was "very good" (Genesis 1:31).

What do you think it means that God saw His own finished work as "very good"? Why not just "good"? One of the reasons creation was "very good" at that point was that it was finished. God had just spent six days creating a home for all living things—as well as a universe to place that home in—and human beings. When He had finished His work, the heavens and the earth and everything that lived in them, were everything He had planned. They were a perfect place for God's most prized creation—you and other humans—to live and multiply.

But what does this mean to you today? Creation happened a long time ago, and some of the things that have happened since then have changed what was once a perfect planet.

Even though creation itself is no longer perfect, it is still a gift directly from God to you today. And one of the first things—if not *the* first thing—you should do when you understand that something is a gift from Him is to give thanks.

Enjoy Creation. . .and Give Thanks

One of the great things about enjoying and studying the wonders of God's creation is that doing these things can remind you of what God is really like in many important ways. For example, when you look up at the stars, planets, and galaxies that are visible from Earth, you can be reminded of just how big and powerful God really is. When you look at the beauty and variety in nature here on Earth, you can be reminded that God likes beauty and variety. And when you look at the amazing detail of your own body, you can be reminded that God made you completely ready to take your place in His carefully constructed plan of creation.

The opportunities to thank and praise God for His works of creation are unlimited. For example, when you go outside and see a beautiful day with lots of sunshine and warmth or a cloudy day with life-sustaining rain, thank God for it! When you see a beautiful woodland area or when you see a desert, a beach, or a valley, give thanks! Or when you see and hear different kinds of birds perching and singing near your home, thank Him for making such a wide array of living things for you to enjoy.

So when you step outside—whether it's light or dark, or whether the sun is shining or it's raining—don't forget to enjoy everything you see around you. And then don't forget to thank the God who made it all happen!

Many towns and cities provide recycling for plastic
bottles, metal cans, and newspapers and cardboard.
You can help by sorting out your throwaways!

Taking Good Care of What God Has Given You

Do you know what the word *stewardship* means? Basically, it means taking good care of something of great value that doesn't really belong to you. It means treating something that belongs to another person the very same way you would treat it if it belonged to you.

Right after God made the first humans, He blessed them and told them, "Be fruitful and multiply. Fill the earth and govern it. Reign over the fish in the sea, the birds in the sky, and all the animals that scurry along the ground" (Genesis 1:28). So in a very real way, God created the universe and the earth for us humans. His plan from the very beginning was to put people in a higher place than all the animals and other living things. We were meant to multiply and to rule over the whole earth!

At the same time, though, the Bible teaches that even though the earth and the things that live here are for our use, they don't really belong to us. Long after God completed the creation of the earth and universe, King David wrote, "The earth is the LORD's, and everything in it. The world and all its people belong to him" (Psalm 24:1). In other words, everything God created—including your own body—belongs to Him!

How does knowing that the whole universe, the whole earth, and all living things that live here on Earth—including you and all other humans—belong to God change how you see them? Even more important, how does it affect the way you treat them?

Sadly, many Christians in the past took the attitude that taking care of the earth wasn't important. But that attitude went against what God specifically told us we should do (take a look at Genesis 1:28 and 2:15). When we damage the earth by neglecting it or overusing it in certain ways, we do harm—sometimes very great harm—to something God created for us and still holds as valuable.

Planting trees is a great way to improve both the beauty and the air quality of your neighborhood.

There are many easy but important ways you can act as a good steward, taking care of what God has given you. For example, when you go out hiking, camping, or fishing, you can make sure you pick up after yourself before you go home. Don't leave anything behind that doesn't belong there. At home you can encourage your family members to conserve energy by turning off lights when they leave the room and by not leaving televisions and radios running when someone isn't watching or listening. If you haven't been doing so already, you can also begin recycling the metal, glass, plastic, and paper you use instead of throwing this material in the trash.

Remember, when you do the things that help preserve the world God created for you, you not only demonstrate good stewardship; you also show God just how much you appreciate all He's done for you—starting with creation itself!